CLASSIC MOTORCYCLES

CLASSIC MOTORCYCLES

GARY JOHNSTONE

BOXTREE

in association with
THE CLASSIC MOTOR CYCLE
CHANNEL FOUR TELEVISION CORPORATION

FRONTISPIECE: **T E Lawrence on his beloved 1935 Brough Superior SS100. Ironically, Lawrence of Arabia killed himself swerving to avoid a butcher's boy on a bicycle in England's leafy lanes.**

First published in Great Britain in 1993 by Boxtree Limited,
Broadwall House, 21 Broadwall, London SE1 9PL

Text © 1993 Gary Johnstone
Photographs © 1993 *The Classic Motor Cycle*
(With the exception of the following: p.58 – Charles Birchmore; p.65 – Mick Walker;
pp.128, 139 – Honda (U.K.); pp.132, 133, 135, 137 – Graham Blunden, The Vintage Japanese
Motorcycle Club; p.140 – Mitsui Yamaha)

1 3 5 7 9 10 8 6 4 2

Designed by Bill Mason
Printed and bound in Italy by LEGO s.p.a.

A CIP entry for this book is available from the British Library.

ISBN 1 85283 452 8

Classic Motorcycles accompanies the Channel Four series
'Classic Motorcycles'
produced by Uden Associates

CONTENTS

ACKNOWLEDGEMENTS

A great many people are responsible for making this book, and the Channel Four series which it accompanies, possible. Phillip Tooth and Brian Woolley of *The Classic Motor Cycle* magazine have been a constant source of information, picture ideas and editorial exactitude. James Castle has been my right-hand man for the last year. Patrick Uden, Richard Seymour, Dave Dixon, Stephen Bailey, Mario Colombo and Camilla Deakin have all strongly influenced the ideas of the series and book. Mick Walker, Vic Willoughby, Titch Allen, Glyn Chambers, Sammy Miller, Honda (U.K.), Mitsui Yamaha, Tippets of Surbiton and countless members of the Vintage Motor Cycle Club, the Vintage Japanese Motorcycle Club, the 59 Club, and the Harley Owners Group have all given much, either in providing machines or information.

Thanks also to Graham Hall for years of access to his great collection, and finally to Isobel, Jim and Alice for giving me the time and support I needed to get the job done.

INTRODUCTION

My parents tried to destroy the motorcycle industry. In the UK in 1992, there were 50,000 new registrations of two-wheelers. In 1959, the year I was born, there were 330,000. During his National Service in Aden, my father rode everywhere on a Matchless G3L. My parents started their courting on an Ambassador Scooter. But when I was born, they, of course, wanted a car. The affluence of the 1960s meant that hundreds of thousands of middle-class families like ours could afford a four-wheeler, so they bought a car, and with it social mobility. My sister and I were dragged all round Britain in a way that my parents never were in the 1930s and 1940s. Cars also bought a certain status.

In the early 1970s my pals and I did our best to revive the motorcycle industry. Helped by the oil crisis, the cheap and economical motorcycle came back into vogue. We duly obliged by consuming all manner of mad Japanese two-strokes. My first "restoration" was of a Yamaha YS5E made from two

ABOVE: It's fun darling, but where will Junior sit?

bikes, one with a busted engine and the other with a bent frame. It was supposed to do 112 km/h and 190 km to the gallon. I recall getting up to a lavish 100 km/h on the bypass, on a downward incline with a following wind. Barry Sheene was not as worried as I had hoped; I might as well have been on a 1919 Model H Triumph.

And that is the point. The motorcycle did not develop very much between 1920 and 1970. It is such an economic lightweight that the least bit of cold financial headwind stops its progress. When things warm up, when there is money about, everyone buys cars. People do not like getting cold and wet, so prosperity brings a paradoxical drop in motorcycle sales. This in turn means that little research and development gets done. In times of hardship, while sales may increase, the product has to be affordable. Again, little research and development is undertaken. Motorcycles bear all the scars and glories of the economies that made them.

The motorcycle, in market terms, is, and probably always will be, a niche product. As such, strange things happen to it which bestow on it an extraordinary magnetism. It attracts users who like its minority "outsider" status. It is for the "one per cent" who want to be different and who will tolerate discomfort to be so. And to appeal to people who like to be different there has to be great variety within the species. Riding a Harley-Davidson, a Ducati, a Triumph or a Honda Fireblade is making a very particular statement. Breeding, cultural nuances, performance differences and design histories all become precious commodities seized on by riders and designers alike.

The definition of "classic" when applied to a motorcycle is an elusive one. A classic motorcycle is often taken to be a machine of outstanding design and engineering merit which has stood the test of public scrutiny and time – this is quite a broad definition and one which provokes no end of argument. It also has to include notions of cult status and the popular classic, oscillating between the two. And it must distinguish itself from the merely old – nostalgia is a sneaky enemy.

Classic motorcycles, then, are *very* different. They are the best of an élite bunch, the essence of the specific breed. They are like totems of the cultures that produced them, rare objects that tell a story. That story is heritage, a key element in every classic, and heritage implies uniqueness, a stamp of originality. The appeal of classics to collectors is that they transmit special and complex messages about what they stand for, why and how they were created. A collector reads a classic machine like an art historian reads a sculpture.

The collector's aesthetic sense of the object has to wrestle with the popular image of the motorcycle as a dangerous toy for macho males locked in adolescence. In fact, it is very hard to separate the two. The macho element creates a particular market demand that feeds back into design and the whole thing becomes a self-perpetuating myth. The Lone Hero, the Gladiator, and the Rebel are all obvious clichés, favourite subtexts for many an advertisement and media gimmick. The static motorcycle is often cast as the caged but untameable wild animal, a beast lurking in the dark, quietly growling. The warrior, half-seen, slips quietly up to the monster's lair. He opens the creaking door and before him, hazy light spreads across the steed – at once both hideous and awesome, mighty and beautiful. The beast dares the warrior to a duel. The man steps forward, and brandishing a shining key, gives the metal Pegasus life. The rider and motorbike exit from a suburban garage, he to tame the wild beast on the open primeval plains, tugging and grappling with its boundless energy on a windswept road in a featureless countryside. Pausing only briefly to telephone his girlfriend to excuse himself, the rider heads off on the infinite road – valiant and heroic. Or some variation thereof. The point being made is always the same - you are free, you are not one of the herd, you have conquered fear on the evolutionary plain and beaten God in a game of chance.

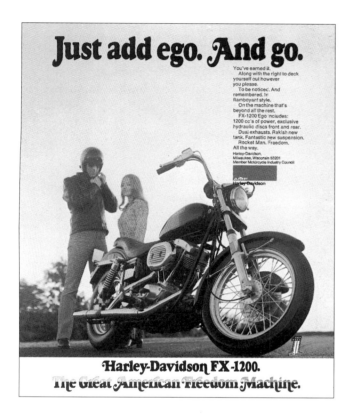

Just add ego. And go.

You've earned it.
Along with the right to deck yourself out however you please.
To be noticed. And remembered. In flamboyant style.
On the machine that's beyond all the rest.
FX-1200 Ego includes: 1200 cc's of power, exclusive hydraulic discs front and rear.
Dual exhausts. Rakish new tank. Fantastic new suspension. Rocket Man. Freedom.
All the way.
Harley-Davidson, Milwaukee, Wisconsin 53201
Member Motorcycle Industry Council

Harley-Davidson FX-1200.
The Great American Freedom Machine.

LEFT: **A penis-extension? No, I just use it to get to work.**

Even watered-down, more middle-of-the-road attempts by the Japanese to introduce motorcycling to a wider public still have to emphasize its difference. You can get around, be free and easy on a nice clean motorcycle – a statement that sets it apart from the crowd.

However, amidst all the sexist and power-obsessed images of motorcycling it is possible to find a much more universal and modernist quality which all motorcycles share and which is bursting out of the great classics. They are pure twentieth century. One can argue with classic enthusiasts about the dangers and inconveniences of motor-cycling till the cows come home; it will have no effect. You can call them sentimental, but you would be wrong. They like motorcycles because in their very metal they possess the essence of our era, and what previous eras had little experience of – speed, possession of a sophisticated material object and the right to be in control of one's own destiny.

Classic Motorcycles, therefore, has a fairly wide scope. It is a critical celebration of motorcycling and of the world's great motorcycles. However, it is not an exhaustive anthology of every machine worthy of the epithet "classic". There are many great tomes and monographs on individual machines and histories of marques. There are also many enthusiastic and powerful testimonies to the particular joy that is motorcycling. This book sits between the two. Its concern is the way that functional, inanimate objects can take on exciting qualities such as character, personality and classic status. What is it that gives a great motorcycle such powerful attraction? Why are different countries' motorcycles so different from one another? Why are Italian machines so light and flighty, Americans so heavy and long-legged, the British so functional and aggressive, the Japanese so smoothly flashy and the Germans so solidly restrained? These national characteristics are not accidental, but the result of differing evolutionary pressures.

Classic Motorcycles is a historical journey to find the cultural and social roots of these special qualities.

The moon is full, the air is clear; the stars are a soft blanket over the hard monochrome countryside. The distant noise of a speeding internal combustion engine breaks through the silence. A single yellow light, moving quickly, picks out trees, hedges and fences and momentarily gives them life. Suddenly, the machine is nearby; a flicker of incandescent acetylene, a whiff of burning Wakefield's Castrol, petrol in the air, a huge, flapping leather coat and flying goggles, a triumphant shout. Here, and then suddenly gone – your first motorcycle.

Right from the start the motorcycle proclaimed itself as an energetic free spirit. By the mid-1920s, while it was still only within the reach of a small proportion of the population, the motorcycle was more prevalent than the car. The average person's introduction to the internal combustion engine was the motorcycle. Often with sidecar, it provided flexible personal transport for individuals at an increasingly affordable price. In Britain, in 1920,

ABOVE: **The genesis of our rowdy image.**

OPPOSITE: **This 1903 pair seem to be having fun, until you look closely and see that the wheels aren't turning. How did they get the dust, then?**

there were 200,000 cars in use, compared to 260,000 motorcycles. Street scenes in period television dramas that show a handful of 1920s cars, with only the occasional motorcycle pottering along, are inaccurate.

The mass-consumption of motorcycles in the early 1920s had come about as the culmination of a series of cataclysmic social changes which had their inception around 1900.

In the late 1800s, 80 per cent of Britain's population lived in towns. To relieve overcrowding and the endemic poverty of industrial centres, massive building programmes were undertaken in outlying areas. To move to the outskirts was the great aspiration of the day. If you were working class, you lived in the town centre; the lower-middle class lived on the periphery, and the upper-middle class inhabited the new outer suburbs (places such as Leyton, Willesden, Pinner, Croydon), quickly dubbed Metroland. The aristocracy stayed in their rightful, socially mobile

spots; bureaucrats could travel around the country enforcing standards. The regulation of daily life around steam mechanization, keeping to the schedule, became the norm. The railway engine of 1900 was the pinnacle of technological endeavour. But it was also a despot, guilty of the crime of monotony.

Meanwhile, town centres were still dominated by the horse. It pulled delivery carts, small and large buses, trams and private coaches. The streets were clogged and filthy. Suburbia must have seemed idyllic by comparison.

Despite the initial attractions of the respectable, secure and sedate suburban life, there was an inchoate and growing desire for travel. Most families had rural roots of only a few generations back. The folk memory of the nation was of green and pleasant lands. The trend towards rediscovering the countryside, which was to flourish after the First World War, was starting to take hold. The expectant populations of the new century were hungry to explore horizons beyond the rails.

While many walked into the leafy lanes surrounding suburbia, others pedalled. The rear-chain safety bicycle was the first mass-produced consumer durable to be within reach of the working class. The bicycle was astoundingly popular in the late 1800s and early 1900s. By 1920, bicycle sales had reached 3 million in Britain alone. Many cycling clubs were formed and racing became a widespread obsession. Velodromes, circular board race tracks, sprang up all over Britain, France and the USA. Professional racers fought it out in front

position as both landed gentry and townhouse dwellers.

As a result, the need for daily transportation expanded greatly. The train flourished. and Britain became a railway state – rigid, predictable, regular as clockwork. Day after day, the train herded human beings between the frozen poles of the workplace and the respectable cul-de-sac dwelling. Commuting was born.

This, however, was to be the railway's swansong. Steam-powered transport had annihilated distance; the "Fourth Estate" had opened up Europe and America. But the emergence of new forms of transport brings with it great political change, and the train brought nations under central control. Armies could be quickly despatched to trouble

ABOVE: **The 1887 Butler. Britain's first petrol-powered vehicle featured a twin-cylinder, watercooled engine with clutch, jet carburettor and electric ignition.**

OPPOSITE: **The 1885 Daimler and Maybach.**

of capacity, heavy-betting crowds from Paris, through Canning Town to New York's Madison Square Garden. Specialist periodicals fed the public news of the latest technological innovations. By the late 1890s, they were starting to report on experiments with powered machines.

The arrival of the petrol engine was one of the many exotic discoveries that fuelled the heady optimism of fin-de-siècle culture. Most people's sedentary occupations and lifestyles were enlivened by a staple diet of magazine images of marvellous fantasy inventions like time-travel and great adventures into the unknown. The power of new technologies such as electricity to cure the great many social ills of the day seemed unlimited. The internal combustion engine quickly became *the* symbol of engineering prowess. It attracted a whole gaggle of adventurous engineers and over-confident entrepreneurs. It caught their ambitious imaginations. The reality of their creations was a lot less impressive. The early years were marked by a chaos of design.

The German Dr Nikolaus August Otto invented the four-stroke internal combustion engine in 1876. His talented assistant Gottlieb Daimler patented an engine in 1884 which could develop 800 revolutions per minute. With his partner, Wilhelm Maybach, he produced a powered bicycle in 1885. The machine was basically half a horseless carriage with wood and iron wheels. Two years later, in England, Edward Butler made a tricycle which had a twin-cylinder, two-stroke engine with

rotary valves (a feature the Japanese made a fuss about in the 1970s).

Until this time, every invention had been very experimental and isolated. Practical men, engineers, were essentially working alone to crack a vaguely understood nut. Like their ancestors in the field of steam, there was little theorizing before invention. Often the understanding happened long after the machinery had proved itself a commercial success.

The first commercially available machines did not happen along until 1896. Hildebrand and Wolfmuller of Munich made a two-cylinder, four-stroke which was capable of 24 mph, and quite a few were sold. Colonel Holden in England made a four-cylinder, watercooled machine which sold for three years. In 1899, the Waltham Manufacturing Company of Massachusetts, offered the Orient-Aster Motor Cycle for sale.

Although Britain and the USA were soon to be the great motorcycling nations of the pioneer period, it was France which became the very first centre of motorcycling excellence. This was due solely to the pre-eminence of the De Dion Bouton company. Count de Dion and his older working-class partner Georges Bouton were the perennial aristocrat enthusiast and horny-handed-son-of-toil partnership. De Dion was twice as tall as the diminutive Bouton. Together they designed and manufactured a series of small, light petrol engines which flooded the world market and became the archetypal design for many years. The widespread

commercial availability of their engines started the trend of attaching engines to bicycles. De Dion Bouton opened up motorcycle manufacture to the large number of would-be entrepreneurs and engineers. Their engines were used and copied by virtually every manufacturer imaginable. Even Oscar Hedstrom produced a De Dion copy for his first Indian motorcycle. All of this was done with scant regard for international patents. The Japanese were not the first in the world of motorcycling to be accused of copying.

Many forces, therefore, created fertile conditions for the first petrol motorcycles: the desire for unrestricted travel, the cyclist's wish for powered assistance, widespread faith in technology and the comparative reliability of the machinery. The trouble was that no one knew what a car or a motorbike should look like. Many existing vehicle types, such as horse carriages and bicycles, simply had some form of petrol power lashed onto them. In fact, it would not be untrue to say that there was a rush to marry the lightweight engine to the bicycle.

The 1898 Werner is typical of the first precarious two-wheelers; a small De Dion Bouton-type engine clipped to the frame of a standard bicycle. A petrol and oil tank hung from the cross bar. A wheel was modified to take a pulley and connected to the engine by a twisted leather belt.

The important point to note is that the motorcycle's predecessor was the bicycle; it was never a two-wheeled version of the car. Pedal and

RIGHT: Though the proprietary De Dion engine became almost ubiquitous amongst early motorcycle manufacturers, the firm of De Dion Bouton had done most of their development work on tricycles with the engine geared directly to the rear axle.

motorcycles shared the same magazines and peri-odicals for a few years until the publication of the first edition of *The Motor Cycle* in March 1903. (*Motor Cycling* made a brief appearance in 1901 and was relaunched in 1910). The maelstrom of

ABOVE: The "solution" at last. The 1903 Werner.

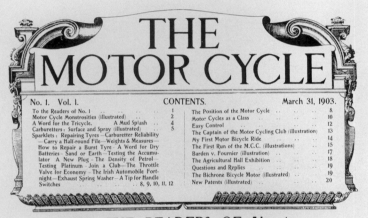

THE MOTOR CYCLE

No. 1. Vol. I.   CONTENTS.   March 31, 1903.

TO THE READERS OF No. 1.

A S a rule the first number of a new paper is accompanied by some sort of introductory explanation, we might almost say excuse, for its existence, but *The Motor Cycle* enjoys an exceptional advantage in this respect, as it has been established in response to a very widely-expressed desire. At the present time there is no journal which deals wholly and solely with the motor cycle and motor cycling, and this is the gap we have decided to fill in response to the general request to which we have just referred.

Motor cycling as a pastime is now firmly established, and its votaries are sufficiently numerous to claim a journal devoted entirely to the special subjects of interest to them. In its early days motor cycling was regarded either as a special branch of cycling or motorcaring ; but it has developed so rapidly that it is impossible to deal with it adequately in a cycle or autocar publication, as there are many people within the ranks of motor cyclists who are not much interested in pedal cycles, and who are well aware that the motor car, even in its most inexpensive form, is entirely beyond their reach from a monetary point of view.

The main points of the policy of *The Motor Cycle* will be :

(1.) To give practical and useful information to motor cyclists.

(2.) To explain the working of the motor and every part of the machine in the clearest possible manner.

(3.) To describe new inventions and improvements.

(4.) To record all matters of interest in the motor cycle world.

(5.) To promote the exchange of ideas and useful information between motor cyclists.

(6.) To reply to queries. (*See page 19.*)

(7.) To help the motor cyclist to get the utmost enjoyment from the pastime.

(8.) To bear in mind that many motor cyclists are not in receipt of large incomes.

(9.) To foster motor cycling in every possible way. We say nothing about assisting in the development of the industry of motor cycle building, as it is agreed by all who understand the subject that the strengthening and fostering of the pastime must of necessity benefit the industry.

We do not believe in making great claims or promises, as we hope that *The Motor Cycle* and its policy, which we have attempted briefly to outline, will appeal at once to votaries of the pastime. It will not be our fault if this is not the case, and we shall always welcome suggestions from our readers. Whether they can be adopted or not, they will be none the less appreciated, and it will be our constant effort to improve and strengthen the paper in every possible way, so as to ensure its being more and more acceptable to its readers.

No. 1 necessarily lacks certain features which will characterise later issues ; but we have determined to abstain from the objectionable practice too often followed of using "dummy" letters, queries, etc., so as to make a paper complete from No. 1. These features will develop naturally with the paper. They will not be simulated, but they will be heartily encouraged, as we believe them to be some of the most important sections of a medium devoted to the encouragement of a new pastime, and we feel **sure** we can depend on the cordial co-operation of our readers in these matters.

advertisements for new machines, engines, tyres, accessories, clothing and second-hand motor-cycles attests to the sophistication of the fledgling and independent market.

Editorially, the first edition of *The Motor Cycle* paints a different picture. There was wide criticism of many of the commercially available designs, and serious doubt was cast over the permanency of motorcycling itself. What is apparent is the exclusive and up-market nature of the whole enterprise. At a time when the huge bulk of the middle class were paying around £30–£50 per annum on house rent, the 1903 Werner is offered at the attractive price of £45. If you were a bit short of cash, though, how about this used model: "Minerva 1¼ hp Motor cycle, with chain-drive, for disposal; £15; or exchange good typewriter and cash, or

ABOVE: A watercooled, four-cylinder Belgian FN shortly after some redesign by the First World War.

well-bred Great Dane or Bulldog – Forster, Neville's Cross, Durham."

The pioneer motorcyclist, then, was usually well off. They also had to be willing to put up with a fair amount of physical punishment. The machines were extremely impractical; they were virtually impossible to start and broke down with determined regularity. The roads were pot-holed dirt tracks, strewn with horseshoe nails. Puncture repair was a required skill. The general lack of basics, like petrol and oil, meant a great deal of time had to be spent ordering by post. When the motor-cycle did perform, the experience was marked by intense vibration due to the lack of suspension. To add to all this, the rider's body temperature swung violently in every kind of weather. The well-clad, waterproofed rider would lather up after an agoniz-ing push on steep hills. The lightly clad chap would freeze at speed. The ideal constitution was essentially the athletic public-school fellow. In *Reminiscences of Motor Cycling*, Ixion states:

BELOW: This 3½ hp 1903 Alert of Coventry is clearly little more than a bicycle with clip-on engine.

...we were incomprehensible lunatics. Our weird hobby seemed without excuse or justification: it veneered us with a permanent grime which exceeded every known form of filth alike in squalor and in adhesiveness. The uncertainty of being able to start on a journey was only exceeded by the improbability of our ever reaching our desti-nation in the saddle. There were no garages; the longest push could only bring us to the door of some ambitious cycle repairer, more ignorant and less cautious than ourselves. A new machine might

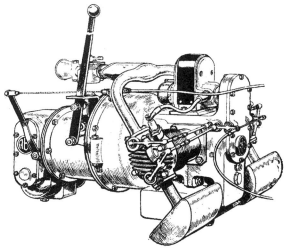

LEFT: The revolutionary 1918 design ABC engine. The transversely-mounted, flat twin predates the BMW by some five years.

RIGHT: The 1000 cc JAP engine in a 1914 Zenith Gradua. Note the external pushrods and manual oil pump on the side of the tank.

easily cost £75 to buy. Its repair bill was long enough to stagger a munitions magnate. The most sympathetic student of human nature might be pardoned for comparing us to the gentleman who carried a slice of toast with him under the impression that he was a poached egg.

All machines possess a supernatural quality. They are imbued with their persona by their creators and as such they are assimilated by society. The motorcycle's animus as a manic, wild outsider seems to have been set from the very beginning. Its madcap invention status and the physicality it demanded meant that it filled the cultural gap left by the young cad's stallion. The public's image of motorcyclists as horse-frightening, over-exuberant young gentlemen was set in those early days, and little has happened since to change that, except that the whole thing has gone downmarket.

While motorcycling was almost exclusively a male activity, there was an upper-class edict that stated that "spunky, rich, young gels could have a bash". In the 1903 May edition of *The Motor Cycle*, Mrs Edward Kennard exhorts her sex: "Wake Up Ladies". She notes that many manufacturers now make ladies' models with step-through frames and dress guards. She blames women for a lack of enterprise and proclaims that the occasional(!) mechanical mishap can usually be corrected even by a member of the fair sex. In the highly sexually divided world of 1903, one can only presume that femininity would seriously have been compromised by the many indignities imposed by motorcycles.

The dangers were great. The reports of accidents were numerous, the most notable and painful being the collapse of front forks at speed. Another treat on coming to an abrupt halt after slipping on the hopeless roads was the immediate combustion of spilt fuel. The hazards of early motorcycling meant that spurious male barriers were raised which have yet to fall.

The industry had work to do if it was going to achieve any kind of permanency for its product. Customers wanted improvements, yet fundamental design problems were only being solved by trial and error. The situation was complicated by numerous shady entrepreneurs responsible for a plethora of dodgy machinery. Mechanical ignorance usually meant premature bankruptcy for most of those involved. E J Pennington, an American who arrived in England in 1896 from Trenton, New Jersey claimed he had patents for many wonderful machines. He made one or two prototypes and then sold the patents to a speculator, Harry Lawson, for

BELOW: The seductive 1898 Pennington – would you buy a motorcycle from this man?

£100,000. Lawson's company, the Great Horseless Carriage Co, subsequently collapsed.

Despite its eclectic nature and the sizeable problems to be overcome, the world's motorcycle industry had enough momentum to persist. Its amazing speed of growth is confirmed by the number of familiar names which had their births in the pioneer period – Ariel, Norton, Triumph, BSA, Royal Enfield, Harley-Davidson, Matchless, Peugeot, Indian. They were not necessarily the big names then – Chater Lea, Rudge, Zenith, Scott, Sunbeam, P&M, Douglas, Martinsyde, New Imperial, Quadrant, Humber, Wanderer, Rex, NSU, Werner and FN were all popular and doing well. Many of the companies grew out of light manufacturing concerns. Many were arms manufacturers looking to diversify into areas of related expertise. Others were one-man-and-a-shed affairs, building to order in response to grand-sounding advertizing.

The fledgling companies tended to fall into two types. For some, engineering excellence was the goal, the elegant and perfect solution. For others there was the search for reliability which would translate into greater sales. Naturally, the same dichotomy of interest persists today.

The first design problem they were all trying to solve was where to put the engine. Early designs had the engine clipped to the front down tube – for example, the 1903 Clement Garrard. This allowed the retention of the bicycle pedals for use on hillier terrain. Models by Phelon and Humber

ALFRED ANGUS SCOTT

The pioneer period was the time of the archetypical inventor. Working in a garden shed, someone with basic engineering experience could go out and buy himself a lightweight engine and a bicycle and call himself a motorcycle manufacturer. Few, however, really tackled the design problems basic to motorcycles. Most were working on hybrid machines that were a mix of first principles' engineering and bicycle technology. Alfred Scott stands above everyone. He was one of the first designers to sit down and work the thing out from scratch, to design a complete machine. He got it right virtually first time.

In 1908, Alfred Scott took the world by storm. At the start of the Newham Hill Climb competition, while other competitors ran, sweating and puffing, pushing their reluctant machines into action, Alfred sat quietly on his invention waiting his turn. On the starter's orders, he pushed down on his kickstart and took his two-stroke twin to win four gold medals.

Alfred Scott was a Yorkshireman from Bradford. He went to Abbotsholme public school but his family was not particularly

wealthy. He came from a textiles family and worked on the mill machinery before training to become an engineer. After a day's work he would play the piano to relax.

He was a perfectionist. The beauty of the Scott is its simplicity. The engine has very few moving parts. The side panels of the engine are held in place by two metal straps, which are removed by undoing one bolt. The strap is then used to remove the big end. The removal of an engine's big-end bearings is a mighty feat; on a Scott it can be done at the side of the road in minutes. The drive is taken from beside the central flywheel straight to the two-speed gear. The power and handling of the Scott resulted in the team winning two Senior TT races in a four-year period. In 1914, a Scott set a new lap record of 85 km/h (53 mph).

Alfred Scott's tireless experimentation, however, was his downfall. He moved away from motorcycle manufacture, and dabbled with a three-wheeled car design. He died at the early age of forty-eight from pneumonia contracted while indulging in another of his passions – pot-holing.

had the engine replace the front down tube. The 1903 Werner, built in Paris by the two Russian brothers Werner, showed the way forward. The engine was placed low and centrally in a specially constructed frame. The engine replaced the bottom bracket and thus prohibited the inclusion of pedals. The more powerful engine just about compensated for their loss. This engine position gave a low centre of gravity, stability and strength. The idea caught on rapidly.

Engines themselves were starting to evolve. Single-cylinder engines like those in the trusty Triumphs of 1907 were most common. Triumph sought reliability and favoured the relative

OPPOSITE: **A 1914 Indian twin with electric start.**

BELOW: **An FN four-cylinder engine, first designed in 1904.**

mechanical simplicity of the single. Twin-cylinders in V-formation like the Clyno and the Harley-Davidson became common by the mid-1900s. The JAP by J A Prestwich of Tottenham, London was perhaps the most famous. It powered the Zenith, Matchless, Brough Superior and Royal Enfield. Engine sizes also varied considerably. Huge monsters of over 1000 cc (60 cu ins) were often matched in terms of power by machines of under half that size.

No one engine design is ideal for all conditions. Big engines with one cylinder give good top speeds but are difficult to accelerate because of the inertia to be overcome. And they vibrate badly at high engine speeds. However, they can heave their way up out of low speeds without stalling. Keeping the volume the same but doubling the number of cylinders adds mechanical complexity but helps acceleration. Vibration becomes less of a problem. The two pistons balance each other out to a large extent, and this is particularly true when the pistons are horizontally opposed — that is at 180 degrees to each other — as in the Douglas, ABC and most notably BMWs. Some regard this as the most elegant solution to twin-cylinder engine design, although it does make the whole motorcycle either overlong or wide, depending on how you fit the engine.

What you gain on the swings you lose on the roundabouts. With big twins, there is still a lot of inertial mass, which inhibits rapid acceleration, to be overcome. Smaller piston sizes accelerate well, and vibration is less of a problem, but you may end

up with a low top speed, unless you have the guts to go for the mechanical sophistication of four cylinders, the Belgian FN, British Wilkinson and American Indian being the most notable examples. The Belgian FN was one of the first machines to dispense with the bicycle tradition. Its in-line, four-cylinder engine delivered plenty of smooth power through shaft drive to the rear wheel. Its smoothness was further enhanced by parallelogram, twin front fork suspension.

Size and cylinder layout started to differ within certain countries. France and Italy generally preferred small-engined, lightweight, highly manoeuverable machines; Britain liked raw power but not at the expense of handling, so size was generally mid-range; America started to favour size, but did not demand lightning acceleration.

The terrain encountered to some extent determined the design. In the USA, the 1915 Indian is ideally suited to long, straight roads. It's a long machine with beautiful leaf-spring suspension. It has a tall, narrow engine of 998 cc, with inlet-over-exhaust valve layout, three-speed gearbox, twistgrip controls and elegant, swept back handlebars. Its key qualities are comfort and stamina. It needs time to start to pace out. Its engine beats along at a steady clip-clop rhythm, as it eats up the prairie roads. George Brough, the designer of the Brough Superior, once said, "Mankind has a natural partnership with the V-Twin. Its slightly offbeat exhaust note awakes folk memories, for it is akin to the hoofbeats of a galloping horse, and man and

horse have been partners since the dawn of time."

On the other hand, the 1913 Scott is a classic example of a light, powerful English bike built for hacking around twisty green lanes and conquering the toughest terrain. It has a watercooled 450 cc parallel twin-cylinder, two-stroke engine with a two-speed drive.

Tangentially, advances in metallurgy also influenced design. Early engine parts would often burn or shatter; the constant hammering of the hot valves against their seats often made the valve heads fall off, so riders used to carry spares. Stronger metals meant that parts could be made to closer tolerances. Strength led to lighter parts and therefore better performance.

Public phobias and taste affected design. The black and gold paintwork of the Sunbeam motorcycle created an often copied, classic look for motorcycles. It arose out of another of the firm's business interests – the then very popular Japanned-black enamelware.

Even such fundamental functions as oiling systems, for example, evolved to take into account public feeling. The pioneer motorcyclist would have to oil the engine himself every few miles, by pulling out a plunger on the oil tank which, when depressed, delivered a shot of oil to the engine. The rule was: always over-oil, never under-oil. When mechanical pumps began to replace manual pumps, riders still wanted control, so they often regulated the flow by adjusting a needle valve to suit the type of riding they were doing. Later, when

LEFT: A Zenith Gradua coffee-grinder-handle gear system.

pushed the machine to get it started and jumped on; when you stopped, the engine stopped. Even powerful machines faltered on steeper gradients, and without recourse to lower gears which would lighten the load, engine speeds rapidly dropped. To keep the engine from stalling, the rider was forced to lighten the load himself by supplying the euphemistically entitled LPA – Light Pedal Assistance – using the bicycle pedals.

To climb a mile of 1 in 10 gradient demanded tactics in those days. You paused at the foot to cool the engine and overhaul the belt. Then you made a rush. As a rule the belt began to slip. The next phase consisted of standing on the pedals and whirling your legs round in an invisible blur. After a hundred yards of such light exercise, you resembled a dugout Colonel after being kissed in the Strand by an Australian private on Armistice night.

IXION: *Reminiscences of Motorcycling.*

The 1912 Bradbury featured one of the first rudimentary forms of variable gears. The front pulley on the engine could be unscrewed and widened so that the leather belt rode lower in the pulley. The smaller diameter at the front gave a higher ratio, but the belt then had to be shortened by a couple of links to compensate for the slack. This whole procedure had to be performed at the bottom and top of every hill and led to some very sore and dirty hands. This did little to improve the image of the pioneer motorcyclist

pumps were completely capable of doing the job, machines like the 1924 BSA still featured sight glasses so the rider could see the oil was flowing.

Gears, however, developed as a matter of necessity. Initially, the engine and back wheel were linked by a leather belt. There was no clutch. You

OPPOSITE: The 1913 Scott – a machine well ahead of its time.

RACING

The achievements of racing and long-distance trials and their effect on sales was not lost on pioneer manufacturers. Many advertisements proclaimed the great victories. Small-circuit motorcycle racing grew out of velodrome bicycle racing. America loved the sport and many new circuits sprang up in the early 1900s. Jake de Rosier, the famous Indian rider, started off as a racer for George M Hendee's bicycle team. Indian exploited race victories and designer Oscar Hedstrom pushed the technical development of the race machines hard. Speed records were established in 1908 and rose from an average of 109.8 km/h (68.6 mph)to 160 km/h (100 mph) in 1916.

Many individuals attempted feats of endurance and prowess. In Britain, the Land's End to John O'Groats trial became the vogue; the trip was covered in 41½ hours in 1908. Official events soon sprang up. Other countries had their own versions – Paris to Vienna, Paris to Madrid, Milan to Naples.

In 1907, the first Thousand Mile Reliability Trial, later renamed the International Six-Days Trial, was held. The winner was Teddy Hastings, a member of the Crescent Motorcycle Club of the Bronx, New York on an Indian twin. He scored 994 points out of a possible 1,000. This achievement proved the enormous reliability of the Indian and boosted sales internationally.

The ill-fated 1903 Paris to Madrid race prompted the French to organize a race over a closed circuit. The international competition accused the French of cheating and went off to start similar races in their own countries. This led to the creation of some famous events – the Circuito del Lario in Northern Italy and in 1907, the first Isle of Man Tourist Trophy Race, the "TT". Racing was banned on British roads, but the Isle of Man, with its separate government, saw the potential of attracting regular crowds to the holiday isle.

Twenty-five machines were entered for the first TT which was to be held over a distance of 253 km (158 miles). The entries included the JAP-engined Matchlesses of Charlie and Harry Collier and the works Triumphs with Frank Hulbert and Jack Marshall on board. Rem Fowler who had raced for the Rex factory switched to the unfancied and unknown 700 cc (42 cu ins) Peugeot-powered Norton for the twin-cylinder class. The Norton led for the first lap but mechanical failures and a puncture at 100 km/h (60 mph) gave overall victory to Charlie Collier on his single-cylinder Matchless. Collier's average speed was 61.15 km/h (38.22 mph). The speeds rose quickly. In 1909, the average speed of 78 km/h (49 mph) was turned in by Harry Collier's Matchless. In 1910, Charlie and Harry Collier were first and second. The Indian ridden by Jake de Rosier was widely touted to win the 1911 TT. The course was extended to four laps of 60 km (37.5 miles) and included the stiff climb of Snae Fell mountain. A 585 cc Indian twin with three-speed gearbox did win the race with an average speed of 76.2 km/h (47.6 mph), beating the Matchless of Charlie Collier, who was later disqualified, into second place. However, de Rosier was not used to the rough road courses and the winning Indian rider was Englishman Oliver Godfrey.

The anti-climax of not seeing de Rosier and Collier battle it out at the Island meant that their scheduled meeting at the South of England track, Brooklands, was promoted as a major Britain versus America challenge. Brooklands had opened in 1907. It was a purpose-built concrete oval with very steep banking. At speeds of over 128 km/h (80 mph) the two champions battled it out neck-and-neck over three races. De Rosier won the first two-lap race by a length but blew a tyre at 144 km/h (90 mph) in the five-lap event. He won

RIGHT: **Charlie Collier with his 1907 TT-winning Matchless. Behind is his father, H A Collier Senior, founder of Matchless Motorcycles.**

the second two-lap event to establish Indian as the leading machine of the era. The event also established the popular Trans-Atlantic Races.

Scotts fared well and won the TT in 1911 and 1913. After the First World War, a Sunbeam ridden by Tommy de la Hay won the 1920 event with an average speed of 82.37 km/h (51.48 mph). This is a remarkable feat on unsurfaced roads, riding something not much stronger than a bicycle. His top speeds were reaching 144 km/h (90 mph) and he had to brake hard with poor brakes for 16 km/h (10 mph) corners.

The 1920s marked the parting of the ways for Europe and America in road-racing terms. The Europeans developed the Grand Prix format over closed road circuits, while the Americans favoured the specially-built oval tracks. The split was to have great repercussions on the evolution of motorcycle design on both continents.

and presumably did little for successful courting.

Like today, many designs were improved because of racing. The popularity of hill-climb competitions and in particular the Isle of Man Tourist Trophy Race, the TT, with its renowned mountain section, hastened the arrival of multi-speed gearing. The Zenith Gradua had a coffee-grinder handle that, when wound up, opened the front pulley. But instead of having to stop and take a link out of the belt, the coffee grinder moved the rear wheel backwards in the frame to compensate. The Rudge Multi had a lever that, when operated, closed the front pulley and opened the rear wheel pulley, thus altering the ratio and maintaining belt tension.

Chain drive, introduced by Phelon and Rayner, and used by Indian from 1901, was effective but unpopular because of the harshness of the power delivery. Many riders preferred belt driven machines because of the inherent damping, but belts slipped in the wet. Eventually, Royal Enfield patented a rubber shock-absorber for use in the rear wheel, thus damping the shocks from chain drive. Belt drive had faded out by the mid-1920s.

Most machines were supplied or could be fitted with acetylene lights. If properly maintained, acetylene lights worked well and were surprisingly bright. Inside the lamp was a water reservoir which could be opened to release water onto calcium carbide lumps below, to produce acetylene gas. However, convenience meant that the electric light outgrew its more bothersome counterpart. From as early as 1914, Indians had electric starting and lighting.

OPPOSITE: 1915 soldiers exposing the motorcycle to harsh evolutionary pressures.

By 1914, most features of the present-day motorcycle had been tried in some form or other. Many ideas suffered from lack of research and development and the rudimentary nature of basic materials. The good solutions were also spread across a mass of different bikes: 200 manufacturers in USA, 200 in UK, at least 200 in Europe. And the essentially handbuilt motorcycle was still only attainable by the wealthy. However, the proportion of athletic types riding for recreation was diminishing and those using motorcycles for transport was increasing.

That is not to say that riding a typical pioneer motorcycle is anything like riding a contemporary machine. In winter, to free a piston stuck to the cylinder bore by thick oil, and also to provide a rich mixture, you opened a tap on the fuel tank and ran a little neat petrol into the cylinders. You pulled out and depressed a plunger in the oil tank, thus delivering a shot of oil to the engine. You then had to set the ignition-timing lever to full retard. The other two levers – the choke and air – were set to the start position. The compression lever was lifted to raise the exhaust valve and then one started to pedal madly. Once you had got the engine spinning, you dropped the exhaust valve to bring in compression and hopefully the engine would fire. If you had some form of clutch, at this point you lifted the rear stand, put the machine into gear with your right hand and set off. As you rode, you brought the timing lever round to advance. The choke lever had to be adjusted to running setting and the air lever used to vary your speed. The clutch was on the left, the

gear change on the right of the petrol tank, and the engine needed regular squirts of oil with the plunger mounted on the top of the oil tank. Braking had to be planned well in advance.

What really sorted the motorcycle out, unfortunately, was war. War has had the most extraordinary effect on motorcycling and the motorcycle industry throughout its history. The great irony is that it was lack of war in the USA that destroyed the US motorcycle industry. America did not enter the First World War until 1917. While European industry was working flat out to supply its voracious armies, American industry was less diverted. From 1914 to 1917, Ford were able to make great strides in developing the famous mass-production techniques which made their Model T automobile extraordinarily cheap. By the conclusion of hostilities, the US motorcycle manufacturers were starting to lose the price war. When automobile sales volumes expanded there was no chance for the motorcycle. What had been for the two-wheeler a potential mass-market very quickly became a niche market. Such a situation could not support more than a few manufacturers, and suddenly there were dozens of bankruptcies. By the 1920s, only Harley-Davidson and Indian remained as serious contenders in the market. Excelsior and Henderson still existed marginally but were gone by the end of the decade. Indian's production output of 20,000 in 1920 fell to 7,000 the following year.

War had the opposite effect in Europe. Most of

the motorcycle industry had been turned over to war-related manufacture, but a few motorcycle manufacturers, like Triumph and Douglas, managed to get War Office orders for despatch motorcycles. This gave these companies a much bigger manufacturing base and a huge increase in revenue. After the war, many young men had been exposed to motorcycles and had demob pay with which to buy the many army surplus bikes. The summer of 1919 was long and hot and the industry got onto a strong footing. Motorcycling took off in the 1920s. The intense manufacturing and development during the war meant that afterwards manufacturers could offer more manageable and reliable machines. The motorcycle spread down through society, and throughout the troubled 1920s, in the absence of cheap cars, the motorcycle mobilized Britain and much of Europe.

Pioneer motorcycles have a unique quality. They are more than simply relics of a bygone era. They reek of first principles' engineering and are stamped heavily with the personality of their designer. They have a mad energy which must have shocked and excited the intrepid, and inspired the romantic.

The uplift beneath motorcycling in those early days

OPPOSITE: **The modern motorcycle comes of age – a 1928 Norton 16H. The editorial values still need some improvement, however.**

must have been a religion, or we should never have borne its manifold disagreeables as we did. It was derived from three motives. Some of us were engineers; even if we privately regarded the machine as a product of Bedlam, it was certainly an amusing little toy. Others gambled on its commercial possibilities. Others, again, were adventurers, pure and simple. When there is no war on, no filibustering in South America, no uncharted islands to explore, this land of policemen and accurate maps and black coats on Sundays is apt to bore a certain type of temperament. The purchase of a motorcycle imported a spice of risk and uncertainty and Bohemianism into such a life.

IXION: *Reminiscences of Motorcycling.*

By the 1920s the rules of the game had been set. The petrol engine had gained the upper hand over the locomotive. Personal transport was a reality for many. Engineering and entrepreneurialism in manufacturing was starting to find some sort of balance. The 1920s marked the end of doubtful designs like belt drive and acetylene lights. Instead, along came the first really fast motorcycles that handled and stopped well. Motorcycling around the world was heading for its first golden era.

UNION PACIFIC MEETS ROY ROGERS

An endless, straight road undulates gently across the plains of Kansas. On either side, wheat sways in the warm breeze. There is a distant sound of rolling thunder. Under the electric sun, near the horizon, a huge plume of dust rises out of the shimmering heat haze.

In 1910, there were 400,000 km (250,000 miles) of surfaced highway in the United States of America. The surface was granite chips laid on soil and had been neglected for two generations while the train held sway. Everything else was dirt. Pioneer motorcycling on this vast continent was a spine-shuddering experience – mind-numbing vibration from the combination of no suspension and the rutted surface, blurred vision and streaming eyes from the dust. How strong the call of the wild frontier! How strong, for an inspired few, the pull of motorcycling.

The American motorcycle has had to grind its way through this century. Compared to the car, the motorcycle is produced in tiny numbers. It is a

ABOVE: Oscar Hedstrom on an Indian racer in 1904. OPPOSITE: A 1953 1300 cc (80 cu ins) Indian Chief – the last flamboyant flourish before extinction. The acres of bodywork and the custom leatherwear say one thing: "America".

heavily-squeezed market. At the same time, the motorcycle industry means "Good ol' American engineering at its best." Its health is seen as a barometer of the nation's industrial and psychic health. Every minute "error" in design, every bad business decision, has come under microscopic scrutiny. While they were by no means always angels, manufacturers simply have not had even the slightest margin for error. The motorcycle business in the US has had it tough.

The statistics tell the tale. In 1913, before the Great War started to affect production and sales, over 70,000 motorcycles were being produced annually in America. After this profound disruption, the industry looked forward to another era of expansion and innovation. In 1920, there were at least three dozen significant US motorcycle manufacturers. Between them they were beginning to get sales back to pre-war levels. Everything would have been fine for a while, but Henry Ford had other ideas.

1,905,500 cars were produced. By 1929, this figure had peaked at an almighty 4,455,100. The total figure of four-wheelers on the American roads in 1929 was over 26 million. By 1940, the road surface had increased to 2.4 million km (1.5 million miles) in a continent of 5.6 million square km (3.5 million square miles). Against such overwhelming odds, the comparatively smaller motorcycle industry just simply rolled over and waited to die.

Consequently, the American Motorcycle in the 1990s means one thing to the collective consciousness – Harley-Davidsons. They are the sole survivors of a market that used to boast many proud names: ACE, Excelsior, Thor, Indian, Pope, Flying Merkel, Limited, Wagner, Emblem, Hudson, Cyclone, Cleveland, Henderson, Pierce, Reading-Standard – all names familiar to the motorcyclist of the Roaring Twenties. To all intents and purposes, by the end of that decade they were gone, apart from Indian, Excelsior and Harley-Davidson. Excelsior stopped production in 1931, and Indian expired in 1953. Harley-Davidson's solitary existence means that the huge V-twin-engined machine is now as much a part of American culture as Mickey Mouse, Coca-Cola and the Empire State building. In the same way that Vespa means Italy, Harley-Davidson *is* the USA. But Harley-Davidson has had to earn its stripes (red, white, blue, and chrome, of course) the hard way.

The 1920s was an era of gross financial irresponsibility in the US. The causes of this mad spending spree are manifold. One cause is particularly pertinent to the motorcycle industry: in 1914, Henry Ford doubled the wages of his car factory workers from $2.50 to $5.00 per day. It set off a whole round of wage rises which ultimately shook the economically lightweight two-wheel industry. The resultant artificial affluence of the 1920s sent car sales rocketing. It instigated a massive road-building programme and a lasting obsession for leisure motoring. Motels and wayside diners sprang up all over the continent. In 1920,

ABOVE: **Just one of the many casualties – the beautiful Flying Merkel.**

OPPOSITE: **The legendary Jake de Rozier takes it easy for once.**

The many industrial casualties of the car's expansion amounted to a tragic fall after what was an extremely auspicious start. In the pioneer days, the baton of motorcycling excellence was first picked up by the French and quickly passed on to the British who carried it until the 1960s, when the Japanese stole it (or picked it up after it was dropped, depending on your point of view). However, for a handful of years before, and during, the early part of the First World War, some would argue that America was producing the best machines. But at that time, those machines were not Harleys, they were Indians.

Indian was the biggest manufacturer in the early days of American motorcycling. Teddy Hastings' wins in the International Six-Days Trials in 1907 and 1908 (then known as the Thousand Mile Reliability Trial) and the Indian win in the 1911 Isle of Man TT earned them widespread recognition and sales.

Indian was founded by George M Hendee, a bicycling enthusiast, who, after a notable amateur and professional career in racing, became a salesman for a number of East Coast manufacturers. He set up his own bicycle manufacturing business in 1897 in Springfield, Massachusetts. The popularity of indoor board-track cycle racing gave Hendee's competitive energies a further outlet. He trained a young French-Jewish immigrant mechanic as a racer, and together they won many races in New England. The young bicycle racer Jake de Rosier, became one of the great pioneer motorcycle racers. Hendee's successes encouraged him to become a race promoter. In 1900, at the Madison Square Garden Track in New York, he spotted a

much-improved, motorized pacing tandem designed and built by a young Swede, Oscar Hedstrom.

By 1901 Hedstrom, financed by Hendee, had produced a prototype, the first Indian motorcycle. The engine was a single-cylinder design, based on

BOARD RACING

Board racing (on wooden, oval, banked tracks) was immensely popular up until the 1920s. It was big business, but it was also very brutal. Indian star Eddie Hasha (right), like all riders, regularly diced with death while setting world records. On 1 May 1912, he set a mile record at a speed of 95 mph at the Playa del Rey track near Los Angeles. But over the years, the sport became tainted with betting, the sale of "Moonshine" and prostitution. This, plus the orgy of death on the track, led to its eventual downfall. Not before Eddie Hasha was killed, however. In 1921 at Newark Track, New Jersey he and a few other riders flew off the banking killing themselves and a number of spectators.

RIGHT: Crazee! The Indian
Scout is ideal for the Wall
of Death because of its
rock-solid handling.

the De Dion principle, but Hedstrom had redesigned and improved the timing, ignition and carburettion. By the end of 1902, nearly 150 machines had been sold to the public. High-profile advertizing and regular demonstrations by Hedstrom and de Rosier at races and club meetings meant that for 1903 the company had more orders than it could fill. Indian had very quickly become one of the most prominent names in the industry and was about to embark on a Golden Decade. In 1904 they sold 586 machines and in 1905 doubled that to 1,181. By 1913, they were selling over 31,000.

This era of success was driven by the ceaseless and innovative pioneering of Hedstrom and his design team. In 1905, Indians were the first motor-cycles to have twistgrip controls. They had two, in fact: one for the throttle and one for the ignition timing. In the absence of reliable cables, the twist-grip's action was transmitted by an ingenious set of nickel-plated rods linked by universal joints. In that year, Indians also had adjustable, sprung front forks, a luxury when compared to the ubiquitious solid bicycle forks.

Significantly, Hedstrom was also experimenting

that year with an engine design that was to become synonymous with Indian and American motorcycles in general – a 42-degree V-twin.

The V-twin was basically a single with another cylinder grafted onto the crankcase. They were a lot heavier than the singles, but this was not necessarily a disadvantage, as the appalling road surfaces bounced off of lighter bikes anyway. Vibration was a problem, but the best compromise between vibration and adequate power was eventually found to be 1000 cc (60 cu ins). The V-twin is a good design for a motorcycle because it allows high capacity while retaining a narrow profile and a reasonably short wheelbase.

The twin was offered to the public from 1906. It initially had a capacity of 425 cc (26 cu ins) and could easily be fitted to the standard diamond-

BELOW: A 1929 Indian Scout Model 101, 750 cc (45 cu in) version of the much-loved side-valver that kept on chugging from 1920 until 1931.

shaped cycle frame. The machine's supremacy was underlined by a carefully arranged smashing of the Transcontinental Speed Record. Riders Louis J Mueller and Indian's first franchised dealer, George Holden of Springfield, completed the 5,562 km (3,476-mile) trip in 31 days, 12 hours and 15 minutes.

From the early days, Indian made many bikes for law-enforcement agencies. Since then, Indians have featured left-hand throttles. The reason always given was that the police officer could keep his hand on the throttle while shooting his pistol with the right. However, Indian standardized the left-hand control soon after the New York Police, in 1907, bought two Indian twins to catch runaway horses, which were becoming a real danger in the congested metropolis. The speeding cop could use his right hand to grab the reins.

1929 INDIAN FOUR

Before the Second World War, the American landscape could be viewed from the luxurious saddle of an in-line, four-cylinder-engined Indian, introduced in 1927. The ancestry of this machine can be traced right back to the Belgian FN Four, through popular American makes such as the Pierce Arrow, Henderson and ACE. The first Indian Four was actually a rebadged ACE, Indian having acquired the company that year. The 1929 Indian ACE Collegiate Four was essentially a Model 101 Scout with a developed ACE engine.

Development continued apace. By 1908, Indians had mechnically-operated intake valves and magneto ignition. However, in 1909, the racing successes of Jake de Rosier and others brought about the first significant design changes to the production Indians' frame and steering geometry. The result was a machine that truly looked like a modern motorcycle. Gone was the bicycle frame, to be replaced by a loop frame. The fuel was carried in a racing-style torpedo-shaped tank, with separate oil tank. The V-twin now came in two sizes – 1000 cc (61 cu ins) and 625 cc (38 cu ins). The big-lunged V-twin had become firmly planted in the American psyche.

By 1910, Indians were outpacing the competition both in events and design. Many improvements were unseen, like the use of chrome vanadium steel in the frame tubes and forgings. The machines' all-chain drive was supplemented by a two-speed gearbox. By 1911, they had a kickstart.

In 1913, the cheap car was starting to become a reality in the USA, but Indian's orders were still running ahead of production. The management had invested heavily in factory space and equipment and continued their policy of using the best quality materials in manufacture. To protect their investment, Hendee insisted the Indians be offered to customers with even more luxurious developments. Leaf-spring, swinging-arm rear suspension was a huge innovation for the day and, by 1914, electric starting was also on offer.

The year 1913 was a turning-point for Indian, however. The Board of Directors who now controlled the company (Hedstrom and Hendee having become minor shareholders) started to inflate the company's stock values by some dubious practices. The warning bells rang, and Hedstrom resigned to great customer dismay. At the same time, Jake de Rosier, by now an international star, for no apparent reason rode an Excelsior in a scratch race, and Hendee sacked him immediately for disloyalty. De Rosier was injured soon after in a race in Los Angeles and died a year later.

The unifying, highly-directed "boostphase" mentality of Hedstrom and Hendee was ebbing away. The partnership, which had taken the vital and powerful designs of Hedstrom and converted them into strong products tuned to the expectant public's needs, had split. In its place came a remote, often changing board of directors with a hands-off knowledge of product and market. A classic era had drawn to a close.

To the outside world, however, Indian was invincible; its 1913 sales were 31,950 and the company had a market share of 42 per cent. By 1915, the Big Twin was being offered as an all electric model. In addition to electric lighting, the 1915 model had a three-speed gearbox. This machine was a clear head in front of many of its pioneer competitors worldwide.

By 1915, Harley Davidson was a name that was starting to emerge with some force. Harley, up until then, had eschewed competition, preferring to emphasize the comfort, practicality and reliability of their machinery; but the publicity gained from competition was irresistible. Throughout 1915 and 1916, before racing was suspended because of the war, Harley started to eat into Indian's supremacy in all forms of racing.

The Great War was a disaster for Indian. They had a huge commitment to War Department orders – 41,000 machines in all. However, rising costs, set against low, fixed unit costs, meant an overall loss for the period. The company had a huge investment in plant, some of which, like its

RIGHT: The uprated Sport Scout of 1934 design, the machine that won the first Daytona 200 in 1937. This is the 1939 version.

foundry, had to be sold. Dealers, starved of domestic machines, defected to Harley. In addition, Hendee had had enough and resigned in 1916. Massive internal reorganization followed.

Part of the secret of Harley-Davidson's long-term survival, however, was that they came out of the First World War in relatively good shape, having had fewer military duties to perform than other companies. They had also spent the war organizing their dealer network, and came out of the war ready to race. The "Wrecking Crew" of Fred Ludlow, Ralph Hepburn, Albert "Shrimp" Burns, Otto Walker and Leslie "Red" Parkhurst started to clear up on the racetracks of the 1920s.

Indian, while corporately at sea, started the post-war era with the release of the much-loved Scout. The 600 cc (37 cu ins) Scout was made from 1920 to 1931. The secret of its success was its light weight and its peppy performance. Oversized valves meant excellent power development, and in addition, the Scout was very easy to work on. Its practicality meant it was a favourite with the police, while its nimbleness made it a first-class production racer. It took just about every prize going.

Designer Charles Franklin took his invention even further. The seat post was lowered and the frame lengthened to 1.4m (57½ in). With an uprated 750 cc (45 cu ins) engine and better

BELOW: **There were Harleys before Hells Angels. This is a 1904, 400 cc (24 cu ins) single, a gentleman's machine.**

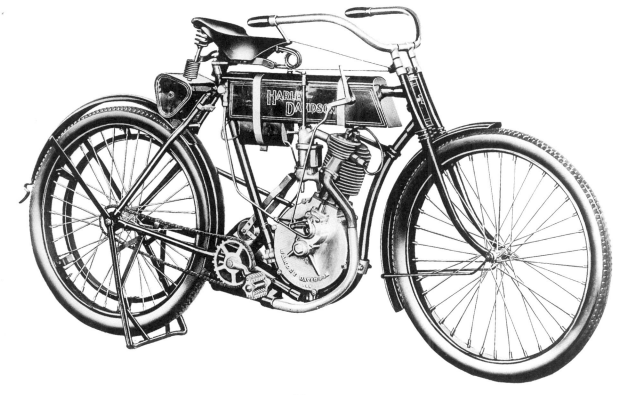

brakes, the new Model 101 Scout was sensational. It was easy to start, and had amazing stability and nimbleness. It became the favourite mount of "Wall of Death" riders and boy-racers. Show-offs used to perform hands-off U-turns in ordinary streets.

In 1922, Indian introduced its first Chief, basically an enlarged Scout with a 1000 cc (61 cu ins) engine and a rigid frame. It was followed in 1923 by a massive 1200 cc (74 cu ins) side-valve version. Chiefs were powerful, capable of over 144 km/h (90 mph), far better than their Harley-Davidson counterpart. But against a backdrop of management resignations, stock market malpractices and lawsuits, the company's fortunes plummeted. In 1929, there were virtually no funds to meet the payroll. In 1930, the chemical giant E Paul du Pont took over Indian.

The 101 was dropped in 1932, to general dismay, and it was replaced by the Standard Scout. The new Scout was an exercise in savage cost-cutting. It was effectively an amalgam of the heavier Chief frame with a 750 cc (45 cu ins) engine. With a poor power-to-weight ratio, customers were unimpressed and sales were poor. The riding public were missing a sporty Indian, and so the factory came up with the Sports Scout in 1934. By the late 1930s, this machine was being used widely in production racing. It had a light, single down-tube frame, coil-spring Girder forks, improved carburettion and alloy cylinder heads. The Sport Scout won the first Daytona 200 in 1937.

Refinement rather than evolution determined

Indian policy thereafter. Both the Scout and the Chief got their renowned skirted fender-styling in 1940. Their rigid frames were also replaced by a plunger-type suspension.

The Second World War dealt another blow to Indian. Initially, expanding order books from the military in Europe and America prompted an increase in Indian production. The company was even starting to amass profits and set them aside for post-war development, but the focus of the war changed to the Pacific and the military cancelled a large number of machines, and refused to pay for them and the already stockpiled parts. Indian's small advantage suddenly evaporated.

Virtually nothing of significance happened to Indians in the following ten years. The machine which the company's fortunes rested on in the 1950s was the ancient Chief. Nevertheless, with their new telescopic Roadmaster front forks, they sold quite well. Extras being offered at the time were reverse gear for sidecar users, radios, fire extinguishers, four-speed gearboxes, first-aid kits, heavy duty tyres, windshields, leg shields and luggage racks.

The full madness of the last dying days of Indian can be seen in the 1953 Chief. It is a monstrous masterpiece: big, wide bars; fat tyres; big leather saddle; a huge 1300 cc (80 cu ins) engine. Like US cars of the 1950s it has tons of styling, with big mudguards and lots of metal. But rather than capitalizing on its solid platform and fearing that American riders might at last desert the V-twin, Indian decided the future was in European-style, lightweight motorcycles. The bikes suffered from a lack of development and poor quality and did not sell. Indian had gone up a wrong turning once too often. After Indian's demise, Harley-Davidson struggled on alone.

The notion of one motorcycle being better adapted to its environment than another might imply that the former is the pinnacle of engineering and design excellence. Often, that is the case. That the Harley-Davidson is truly part of American culture is undoubted. Its mechanical evolution is a function of twentieth-century American economics, geography and politics.

However, looked at dispassionately, this ninety-year-old manufacturer's motorcycles are *not* examples of design genius. In fact, the purist might argue, and argue hard, that the word "classic" cannot be applied to any Harley-Davidson. The necessary quality of design excellence is hard to establish. One might say that they are "agricultural" machines of questionable parentage and expedient design. (Pardon the profanities!) On the other hand, the sheer mass-appeal of Harley-Davidson calls into question the whole definition of the term "classic".

The point is that you *cannot* look at a Harley-Davidson dispassionately. Its cussedness is its charm; its train-like spirit is its allure; its horse's persona is a call to abandonment. Big men fall at its feet; whether its design makes sense or not just does not matter.

It is a bike that only makes sense on a prairie road that stretches straight to the horizon. If you

OPPOSITE: **A 1913, "Silent Gray Fellow" V-twin. Quiet, but powerful. Too powerful for its brakes, in fact, with a top speed in the 50 mph plus region.**

rode a Harley-Davidson round the City of London you would be in for a shock. They do not like tight corners; you have got to sit low in your saddle, cowboy-like, and cruise the Wild West to the rhythmical beat of its massive engine. As Richard Seymour, the designer of the Norton F1 Sport, MZ Skorpion and a fair few Yamahas, says: "...from the waist up the Harley is Roy Rogers, waist down it's Union Pacific."

Red, white and blue. Chrome and Eagles. The American Way. The endless road. The Outlaw. Cruising. Easy Rider. Live to Ride, Ride to Live. And on and on and on and on. The clichés that orbit the Harley-Davidson are enough to make your head spin. You cannot be near one without being suffocated by these massive, icon-laden monsters. They swamp the memory and blur history. What the Harley has got, more than anything, is guts; like a US Marine – stoical, loyal and conservative.

Arthur Davidson and Bill Harley were schoolboy friends from Milwaukee whose parents had emigrated from, respectively, Scotland and England in the 1870s. The two met again after both had worked as apprentices and they shared a common love of fishing. Their idea to create an engine for their rowing boat coincided with meeting a young German, Emil Krüger. Krüger had worked for Aster in Paris and had drawings for a De Dion-type engine. Together, the three came up with a marine engine that worked and it was not long before the fervour surrounding motorcycle manufacture filled their imagination. Arthur and Bill were joined by

LEFT: **A 61E Knucklehead, so-called because of its distinctive rocker covers.**

Arthur's older brother, Walter. Working first from the Davidson family home and then a friend's workshop they had produced a motorized bicycle by early 1903. It was a simple design with a 400 cc (24 cu ins) engine. Later that year, a second machine with a strengthened frame appeared. By 1905, production was eight machines per year and the three founders had a small staff.

This apparently modest start is in contrast to the meteoric rise of Indian, but the Harley-Davidson concern was by no means amateur; Bill Harley was a university-educated engineer. The Harley-Davidson approach was of careful organic growth, without outside investment. They spent a lot of time and effort in the early years testing and improving their product before releasing it to the public. Their ultimate concern, atypical of many contemporaneous manufacturers, was reliability. Consequently, change was slow. The original three-horsepower single remained unchanged in five

years and was the company's only model. Nicknamed the "Silent Gray Fellow", after its paint scheme and long silencer, it was a dependable machine. It was also cheap to run, doing over 59 km to the litre (170 miles to the gallon) under ideal conditions, if you believe the advertisements of the time. In 1909, Bill Harley upgraded the machine, by increasing the capacity to 575 cc (35 cu ins) and adding sprung front forks.

However, Bill Harley was ready to create a legend: the first V-twin Harley. The Model F had its cylinders set at 45 degrees and adopted the generally acknowledged ideal capacity of 1000 cc (60 cu ins). At that capacity, there was a reasonable compromise between power and vibration.

The F was well liked by the public and continued in production for twenty years. It was not until 1912 that the Harley-Davidson started to approach the sophistication of the Indian. That year saw the introduction of a clutch and replacement of the leather-belt transmission with chain drive.

Harley-Davidson entered the war years with production running at around 10,000 machines per annum, about a third of Indian's output. Harley-Davidson's instinctive conservatism meant they also carried a lot less investment in stock and plant. By offering only a modest proportion of their stock to the military (Indian supplied 30,000 war machines, Harley 10,000) Harley kept and indeed expanded their domestic network of dealers and customers, at Indian's expense. As the war ended, both companies were neck and neck, but the Harley star was rising as Indian's was fading.

In the early 1920s, as the full impact of the cheap car hit the industry, both Indian and Harley-Davidson started to buckle. The motorcycle and sidecar combinations they offered were actually more expensive than a Ford Model T. As so often has happened throughout its existence, the motor-cycle was having to make the uneasy metamorpho-sis from a mode of transport back to a luxury leisure item. The American manufacturers were slow to adapt to this changing function.

The sterile climate of the 1920s produced the Harley-Davidson JD, also known as the "74" – a 1200 cc (74 cu ins) version of the J. The Model 9 single had been discontinued since 1918. The only other Harley, a very unpopular flat-twin, the Model W, died in 1922. The American public wanted big V-twins. Ignoring this, in 1926 Harley launched a series of 350 cc (21 cu ins) singles, the Model A and B. They did not sell well. The J and JD V-twins and their variants kept the company ticking over, but the twin-cam models, the JH and JD-H, were considered the best Harleys ever made.

Harley entered the Depression of the 1930s frantically trying to cut costs and eat up Indian's market share. Their approach was short-sighted to say the least. Rather than taking a good look at the market, at what machines were on offer, which ones were selling and what customers wanted, Harley-Davidson looked inside its own four walls and asked, not for the first or last time in motorcycle manu-facturing: "What can we afford to make?" While

1957 HARLEY-DAVIDSON
SPORTSTER

ABOVE: A 1957 Harley-Davidson Sportster, equally at home on or off tarmac.

struggling in a hostile market to sell even trusted machines, Harley introduced the Model C and D.

Both machines were seriously compromised. They were an attempt to make two motorcycles out of one. The C, a 500 cc (30 cu ins) single, had the same frame as the D, a 750 cc (45 cu ins) twin. The C's motor struggled to power the bulky cycle.

BSA ROCKET 3 EXPORT MODEL

Sport fashioned the American machine in many ways. You would expect prairie-crossing machines with their huge gasoline appetites to have big tanks, but the popularity of sport often determined otherwise. In the

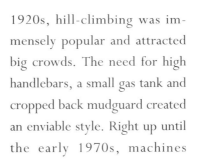

1920s, hill-climbing was immensely popular and attracted big crowds. The need for high handlebars, a small gas tank and cropped back mudguard created an enviable style. Right up until the early 1970s, machines exported to the States from Britain had to have that look. The export BSA Rocket 3 came in a variety of lurid colours, high handlebars and a 2½ gallon pear-drop tank. It did not seem to matter that its range between fuel stops was a paltry 160 km (100 miles).

Similarly, the D's side-valve engine was puny compared to the rival Indian. The 500 cc (30 cu ins) single died in 1937, but the "45" engine, after modification continued until 1953.

In 1929, Harley managed to undermine their reputation further by introducing a replacement for the J series, the VL, which was both heavier and less powerful. The only things which kept Harley alive in this period were an aggressive marketing style and a heavy-handed control of their dealers. Dealers were forbidden to touch, and were often told to destroy, competitors' machines which had been bought in part-exchange.

When the Depression started to hit below the belt, sales for 1933 were 3,300. Dealers were hurting badly, but the initially distrusted 45 and 74 started to gain respect as minor alterations cured

ABOVE: A 1987 FXR Superglide. Its beautifully engineered "Evolution" engine in a basic, trim frame makes a great starting point for customization. Harley have cleverly gone whole hog into the aftermarket accessories business.

the worst of their mechanical problems. The 74 was bored out to 1300 cc (80 cu ins) and it knocked the Indian Chief's ailing reputation further. Innovation, however, continued at a snail's pace. The year 1935 saw the introduction of the buddy seat. Now you could carry a passenger!

The word "Knucklehead" is poetry to a Harley freak. That the Knucklehead nearly destroyed Harley is easily forgotten. The 1936 release of the 61E, with the first overhead inlet and exhaust valves on a Harley, should have been a boost to the company's fortunes but yet again, mechanical shortcomings took the company to the brink. The new valvegear was suspect and had to be hastily redesigned. In all 1,900 machines were recalled for refitting.

Again, by heavy marketing and dealer control, the company narrowly avoided extinction.

Ironically, the 61E has evolved into one of the most sought-after Harleys of all time. It is a true sports bike and at last a Harley which had the measure of Indian. A 1200 cc (74 cu ins) version – the F – underlined the Milwaukee marque's supremacy with a top speed of 160 km/h (100 mph).

As both companies started to sigh with a little relief in the early 1940s, someone decided to get America involved in another world war. Harley produced 88,000 machines for the armed forces, but had 15,000 returned because the war had moved into the Pacific. These motorcycles eventually found their way onto the domestic market. Despite the high turnover of machinery, the prices paid by the military were low and that, combined with the returned machines, meant profits from war production were low. As the war ended, the number of imported motorcycles also rose sharply, aided by relaxed import controls. British middleweights, like the Triumph Speed Twin flooded onto the market in numbers approaching Harley's total output of 15,000 per annum. Typically, the management refused to react. The essential model line of 750 cc (45 cu ins), 1000 cc (61 cu ins) and 1200 (74 cu ins) V-twins stayed.

The Knuckleheads were replaced by Panheads in 1949. Improved overhead valvegear was hidden by a chrome pan on the cylinder head, hence the name. Also in 1949, Harley-Davidson belatedly adopted telescopic forks with hydraulic damping. After experience of the consequences of releasing new features without full testing, one might have expected the factory to have got the front forks right first time; after all, there were plenty of successful designs on the market. But again, improvements had to be made to stop the forks spraying customers with oil when they bottomed out. The "Hydra-Glide", as it was known, eventually took its place in the Harley Hall of Fame, once it had its wrinkles shaken out.

Things hardly improved during the 1950s. In a belated attempt to combat the rising popularity of British bikes, Harley released the K range to universal dismay. The K should have put Harley back into contemporary motorcycling. Gone was the foot-operated clutch and handlever gears; in came, at long last, rear suspension and a completely new unit construction engine. But the cautious manufacturer, after years of overhead valve experience, went back to the ancient side-valve layout.

In 1957, Norton, Triumph, Vincent and BSA ruled the roost on American roads and Harley-Davidson was outgunned. Harley's only assets were tradition, Americanism and, after a period of free testing by the customer, simple reliability. And then, at last, they pulled a big one out of the bag. The XL Sportster arrived and immediately started to "kick some ass". Back came the overhead valvegear; displacement was 883 cc (53 cu ins); the engine had a shorter stroke and a larger bore than its K series ancestor – this Harley could rev! On top of this, it had a pure sports image, *and* it worked. The following year, the XLH and then the XLCH improved the breed greatly. High compression pistons, bigger valves and even gutsier styling pushed Harley out of its trusty old image and into the street wars of the 1960s.

The Outlaw image of the Harley had been born on 4 July 1947, when a gang of Harley-riding wild-boys cruised into the Californian town of Holister and partied all weekend. The supposed outrage and, no doubt, subconscious attraction of this event gave rise to a *Time-Life* spread and a number of 1950s films, like *The Wild Ones*.

Another reason for the change of image from traditional and respectable Cruiser to rubber-burning Hellraiser was the increasing popularity of drag racing. Harleys started shedding weight and private tuners were wringing the last brake horsepower out of the big engines. The chopping up of the bikes blended with the factory's attempts to broaden their range by offering many bolt-on accessories. Customization became central to Harley's spirit. It also underlined the Land of the Free's cult of the individual.

The 1960s was a confused time for Harley-Davidson. They bought the Italian company Aermacchi in an attempt to conquer the light and mid-range market, just when the Japanese were offering similar machines at lower prices and higher specs. By the late 1960s, the company was taken over by Rodney C Gott's conglomerate, AMF. AMF wanted profits and the bikes suffered as a consequence. Hastily installed new equipment and high production targets meant that quality plummeted.

Despite yet another quality control débâcle, Harley was still managing to pump out living legends. The FX "Super Glide", a 1200 cc (74 cu ins) stripped-down sports bike was the ideal base from which to start a personal customization. It was masterminded by designer Willie G Davidson, a committed biker and an inspiring force in the present-day Harley-Davidson organization.

Still, the 1970s were bad for Harley, and by 1980 AMF had bailed out, leaving the company in the hands of a management buyout group headed by engineer Vaughan Beals. Beals has managed to haul Harley back to its present position of growth and stability.

It is precisely because the company has had it so hard that Harley-Davidsons are now so appealing. The lack of enforced evolution has made a machine which still has its roots intact and visible. The Harley was and will always be unashamedly designed for the home market. Dismissal of the needs of other territories is central to its charisma. Cavalier attitudes to feedback from the dealer network and customers in the past have meant that the breed remains relatively pure. A Harley-Davidson is not a hybrid, evolved, complex solution to a set of ever-changing tastes; it is a simple response to a very old problem. So what for a long time looked like bad business now turns out to have been quite good business, if you ignore the near misses.

With Harley-Davidson, you gets what you gets and you had better like it. And if you do not you can always change it yourself.

AVANTI!

Italians are intrigued by the American and British image of the motorcyclist as a greasy, oily, "ne'er-do-well". People in Italy do not see motorcycling in quite the same way as they do elsewhere. Italian motorcycles are treated with considerable respect. Laverda, Ducati, Moto Guzzi, Moto Morini, Gilera, MV Agusta, Aermacchi, Parilla, Cagiva, Aprilia, Bimota – all are revered names. They have status; many of them are old family firms, many of them once state industries. They have more in common with Italian design and fashion houses than with a wider heavy industrial tradition. So classic Italian motorcycles are objects of national pride. Aesthetic creations to be treasured and enjoyed not just by real enthusiasts.

Italian production has been typified by a large number of small manufacturers making many models. Because of their uniqueness, a very large proportion of these machines could be classified as classics. They are too numerous to mention, but all seem to be unified by something quintessentially

ABOVE: **Breath-taking Italian attention to style detail.**

OPPOSITE: **An MV Agusta 750S. Rational thought is not applicable.**

Italian. The Italian classic is something that one can point to but not easily explain. This chapter is an attempt to outline that elusive and exciting quality, highlighting common causes and effects. Many great Italian motorcycles have had to be left out – the Benelli 750 Sei and Aermacchi Ala Verde amongst others – for no other reason than considerations of space.

To the outside world, the Italians have an approach to motorcycle design that defies comprehension. They seem to have a flawed brilliance, the capacity to make a near-perfect motorcycle and turn it into a commercial disaster. They make machines worthy of inclusion in an art gallery, but which do not work very well. They go for glory and court chaos fearlessly.

The MV Agusta 750S is a case in point, an object lesson in how to go bankrupt. Its extravagance made it both an unsellable turkey and, ironically now, a priceless classic.

Until 1971, the best MV had offered the public was a heavy and rather dull four-cylinder, 600 cc

LEFT: These are members of the Carlo Guzzi club who have travelled from Mandello del Lario, on the east bank of Lake Como, to Civenna on the west. Every year on All Soul's Day, motorcyclists from all over North Italy congregate at the church in Civenna, near the site of the Circuito del Lario – the Italian TT course. They go to remember the riders and racers of the past and to mourn friends killed on the roads.

(36 cu ins) tourer. The 750S changed all that. Here at last was a gutsy street-legal racer from Italy. No one believed that the Italians could put something approaching their all-conquering Grand Prix machines on the road. The 750S had an in-line, four-cylinder engine like the Japanese superbikes *and* it had bags of character, something that they lacked. It was the look that was so appealing. Its red, white and blue jelly-mould tank topped off a real prototype image. The red tubular frame and cast alloy engine gave it all the poise of a Ferrari or Maserati. The powerful four leading-shoe front drum brake, megaphone exhausts, clip-on handlebars and rear-set foot pegs said "racetrack". Magazine testers fell over each other for superior

metaphors to describe it. Engineers described it as poetry in metal. The motorcycling public drooled at the mouth, but few had pockets to match their aspirations.

Performance was good with a top speed of 180 km/h (112 mph) at 8,000 rpm. Its racing pedigree was clear. At top speed, handling was excellent and vibration was limited. In town, below 48 km/h (30 mph), it was hard to handle; when idling, the engine sounded like it had a bag of nails churning around inside; in addition, the MV's electrics were a disaster and the chrome fell off. Worst of all, it was nearly three times the cost of a four-cylinder Honda CB750, which had disc brakes and a top speed of over 190 km/h (120 mph).

MV Agusta was ruled by Count Domenico Agusta. Like so many other Italian motorcycle manufacturers, he already had an established family business in aircraft manufacture. He started the motorcycle business in 1945 to try and cash in on the postwar need for cheap transport. The company built a lightweight 98 cc (6 cu ins) two-stroke and went on to become the most successful team of all time in the history of motorcycle Grand Prix racing. They won 37 riders and 38 team World Championships.

Count Agusta's Grand Prix racers had all the regal qualities of thoroughbreds. The 350 cc (21 cu ins) and 500 cc (30 cu ins) in-line, three- and four-cylinder-engined bikes dominated the 1950s and 1960s with such illustrious names on board as Les Graham, John Surtees, Mike Hailwood and Giacomo Agostini.

Grand Prix success dovetailed nicely with the Count's main business of helicopter production. He had a huge contract with the American company, Bell. He was always cautious, though, about the business of commercial motorcycle manufacture. The company offered a small range of lightweight bikes and an ugly 600 cc (36 cu ins) tourer. However, in 1969, against his better judgement, the Count was persuaded by his production team to let them silence the company's critics by building a road bike in the same mould as the Grand Prix racers. Its development and the complexity of turning a Grand Prix motorcycle into a reliable road bike cost the company a fortune.

Pride and vanity made a fearsome machine. The MV Agusta is one of the most distinctive and stylish Italian superbikes ever made. But in a production run of under 2,000, there was simply no profit. The Honda CB750 sold in hundreds of thousands. Frantic cost-cutting on the MV meant an inevitable compromise on ancillaries. Sales suffered. Count Domenico died in 1971 and the already troubled company went through a number of hands until it ceased motorcycle production in 1977. A good 750S, however, may now fetch £25,000.

MV Agusta were just one of the casualties in Italy when the Japanese flooded world markets with cheaper machinery. Since the 1960s, the Italian motorcycle industry has diced with death, trying to compete with the huge investments and mass-production techniques of the Japanese. Their unique, often handcrafted machines, are expensive to make, but this does not deter the Italians.

Ducati, as a motorcycle producer like MV Agusta, rose out of the chaos of post-Second World War Italy. At the time, a great many companies were responding to the call for basic cheap transport. The Bologna company, which had specialized in radio production for the military, turned its idle workforce and damaged factory into producers of a small clip-on bicycle engine.

However, Ducati's reputation abroad is largely based on the designs of their chief engineer, Fabio Taglione. His lightweight single-cylinder and large V-twin machines have always been sought after, despite their high cost. But more so, his name is synonomous with the term "Desmodronic". The valves on most engines are pushed open by a rod or lever and closed by a return spring. At very high engine speeds, the valve can start to float as the spring struggles to reseat it. Performance is obviously affected and it can result in engine damage. In

350 Mark 3 D DESMO

BELOW RIGHT: The Ducati MHR, Mike Hailwood Replica – a stunning machine made in handfuls, to the dismay of the buying public.

a desmodronic engine, the valves are positively closed by the same lever that opens them. This allows the engine to rev a lot faster. In the late 1950s, Taglione's desmodronic race engines won many 125 cc (7 cu ins) Grand Prix. Typically, race engines could be revved to 15,000 rpm without harm.

ABOVE: An engineering marvel: the Ducati MK3D, 350 cc single with desmodronically-driven valves.

Ducati had impressed riders throughout the 1960s with its range of road-going, non-desmo, sporting singles. The 250 cc (15 cu ins) Daytona and its successor, the Mach 1 were the boy-racer's dream. Based closely on Ducati race bikes, the 1965 Mach 1 was capable of over 160 km/h (100 mph)! But in 1968, Taglione went even further and produced a desmodronic single for the road. The 250 and 350 Desmo models, the latter known as the MK3D, were the start of a roadgoing desmodronic legend.

The Ducati MK3D was certainly unique. It was a very slender and attractive bike with a colourful paintjob, but again it was expensive. *Again* the controls and electrics of the bike were skimped. The kickstart, following Ducati fashion, was on the left of the engine, which made starting difficult. (You do not know how weak your left leg is compared to your right until you try to start a Ducati. The only solution is to stand beside the bike, and using your right foot, jump up and then kick down.) And many a Ducati rider, on a dark evening in the 1960s and early 1970s, found themselves with a sudden absence of light. More than a bit frustrating on an otherwise perfect machine; but as the Italians would say: "Who needs lights?"

This side of the Italian character comes from a

BELOW: Hot potatoes! On the left a Ducati Daytona 250, on the right a Ducati Mach 1.

culture where designers are greatly revered. An Italian motorcycle manufacturing company used to be, and in some cases still is, styled more along the lines of a fashion house than a multi-disciplinary engineering works. Costs were high because the manufacturers liked to be unique and used to make the whole bike to the designer's specification. And

while the designer concentrated on the heart of his machine, the ancillaries tended to be rushed or given less attention. This is a contrast to present-day Japanese manufacturing, or the old British approach where you would always have one designer or outside supplier responsible for making gearboxes, one for the construction of the engine and one for designing suspension systems. Mass-produced pieces were much cheaper.

Reliability was a key factor and the sales of Ducati singles struggled to compete against similar lightweight Japanese machinery. Ducati decided, as the British did, that their market should be the superbike category. In the late 1960s, Taglione was asked to produce a 750 cc (45 cu ins) machine. The result was a lineage of heart-stopping, brutally good motorcycles. Taglione, through deference to cost-effectiveness and simplicity of design, came up with a V-twin version of the Ducati single. Unlike a Harley-Davidson's 45-degree cylinder layout, the Ducati 750 GT had its cylinders set at 90 degrees. The front cylinder was inclined forward to a near horizontal position. The result was even cooling of both cylinders and a very narrow profile. The most noticeable feature of the V-twin engine, though, was its exceptionally high quality engineering.

Wisely, the factory backed up the appearance of this machine with an effective race presence. The V-twins won the 1972 Imola 200-Miles against all expectations. The GT was followed by a even more powerful version, the 750 Sport. A tourer, the 860GTI, came out in 1973. The factory also offered a beautiful handbuilt 750SS Imola Replica. However, a series of bad judgements by management led to breaks in the availability of the machines, just when the public wanted them most. The 900SS, the most desirable, was made in strictly limited numbers; customers queued up for their sports bikes and Ducati turned out handfuls.

However, in 1978, one man kickstarted a Ducati renaissance – Mike Hailwood. The multiple world champion had retired from racing after a spell in Formula 1 cars in 1974. This diversion ended in severe damage to his legs, but after a short period in South Africa and New Zealand he was restless. His comeback was spectacular. On a Ducati 864 cc (52 cu ins) V-twin, he stormed to victory in the Isle of Man Formula 1 TT. The next year Ducati brought out the MHR, the Mike Hailwood Replica. Queues formed again but the factory still produced the machine in small numbers. Nevertheless, the publicity gained created a long-lasting wave of enthusiasm which has carried Ducati into its present era of successful production. With new ownership, management and a fleet of race-honed machinery, featuring belt-driven desmodronic valvegear on offer, the marque goes from strength to strength.

While one, as a customer and no doubt as an investor, can be indignant about management shortcomings such as that of Ducati in the 1970s, these problems do contribute to the mystique. The intrusion of personal foibles, be they the designer's or the producer's, all find their way into the metal, sooner or later. Rarity is a prized attribute.

Italy also imbues her motorcycles with a certain quality. The popularity of road racing and the geography encountered – the tight, twisting, hilly roads of North Italy – has created a predominance of light, manoeuverable bikes with good brakes. In a world

motorcycle culture which for the last twenty years has thrown the spotlight on superbikes, small Italian sports classics are a reminder that motorcycling is supposed to be fun. For example, the Moto Morini Settebello 175 of 1957 developed a perky 20 hp – very good for its size. Its high-compression single

RIGHT: The moment the late Mike Hailwood let the clutch out on his Ducati at the start of the 1978 Formula 1 TT, which he went on to win. It was the greatest comeback in the history of motorcycle racing.

LAVERDA 1000 SFC

Last of the great Laverda triples, from 1984, the 1000 SFC had been intended as a limited production run of 200, but production stumbled on through the late 1980s. Its predecessor, the legendary Laverda 750 SFC of the early 1970s, was a classic from the moment the first one came out of the box — a purpose-built, endurance racer sold for road use, the only difference being the inclusion of a horn and number plates. The later 1000 SFC (shown here in 1986 version) was an attempt to cash in on the name. Laverda's financial troubles in the early 1990s led to a company take-over by an Italian businessman who then stripped it of its assets.

cylinder let out a rasping sound that was more familiar on the track than the road. As a road bike it was made in a limited edition — between 800 and 900 motorcycles in a period of two years. Consequently, it is now a very rare machine and much sought after in Italy as well as abroad.

Alfonso Morini was a fanatical card-player and named many of his machines after cards — Settebello means "the seven of diamonds". The motorcycle played unashamedly to the racing emotions of its

OPPOSITE ABOVE: The Italian boy-racer's dream, the impish, highly-collectable Moto Morini Settebello.

OPPOSITE: The modern, popular Italian classic, the Moto Guzzi Le Mans, in 1000 cc form.

customers. It left the factory with clip-on racing handlebars, tuned engine, big Dell'Orto carburettor, lightweight wheels and powerful brakes. It was ideally suited to blasting around the tight Italian streets and up into the twisting mountain roads. Many were used as hill-climb racers, and they earned the factory much recognition worldwide.

The Settebello is typical of Italian bikes of the 1950s and 1960s. They were brilliantly designed to give near-race performance — well-engineered, oil-tight and reliable. And they were produced, like the latest fashions, in small numbers. Pride in creation was more important than money. This is what really shapes the Italian classic – passion. Passion for the object and not the business. You build the bike because you can and you want to. It is that intensity of feeling that the makers and riders share. But it is also a mad hunger that is difficult to combine with running a successful business. It is possible to get into a financial trap. Nowhere is this

more clearly seen than at Moto Guzzi.

Moto Guzzi is one of Italy's most loved marques. The 1000 cc (60 cu ins) Moto Guzzi Daytona is one of the pinnacles of contemporary Italian motorcycling engineering. While it performs on a par with the best Japanese superbikes, it has to wrench its power out of a very basic engine design. The Daytona, like the Ducati V-twin, has two cylinders set at 90 degrees, but they are mounted transversely, so that they stick out either side of the bike into the airstream.

Moto Guzzi has been churning out classics for over seventy years. The Norge, Corsa, Egretta, Ardetta, Alce, Albatros, Airone, Dondolino, Gambalunga, Falcone, Zigolo, Lodola, Stornello, Monza, Imola, California, Le Mans – all are names that inspire the Italian classic enthusiast. They evoke dreams of flight, freedom and glory. Moto Guzzi clearly put passion into their machines, yet, commercially, they have stuck doggedly to two basic four-stroke engine designs – a horizontally

mounted single-cylinder and the transversely mounted V-twin like that in the Daytona – despite some dabbling in two-strokes. Radical change has not been a hallmark of Moto Guzzi's latter years. Indeed, the Daytona is the result of an initially private, four-valve head project by an American dentist and race tuner, "Dr John". Fortunately, the factory picked up this idea and now make the machine commercially under Dr John's guidance.

The first Moto Guzzis appeared in 1921. They were designed by a young Italian Air Service mechanic, Carlo Guzzi, who came from a small fishing village on the east-bank of Lake Como, Mandello del Lario. Mandello is now one of the spiritual homes of Italian motorcycling. The Circuito Del Lario, the Italian TT course, is on the other side of the lake, and many of the other great manufacturers are close by.

Guzzi's design was radical for the time. The single 500 cc (30 cu ins) cylinder lay flat so that the cylinder head was directly and evenly cooled by the passing air. The motor had a large external flywheel which greatly reduced vibration and an integrated crankcase which contained the clutch and gears. The last feature meant only one lubrication system was needed. Lubrication was further assisted by the fact that the engine ran backwards with respect to the wheels. This meant oil was thrown up onto the top of the cylinder and fell down onto the bottom side.

There has been much debate about the handling problems caused by the gyroscopic effects of a

8 kg (17 lb) flywheel turning against the direction of wheel travel. Theoretically, the flywheel would act against the rider's attempt to bank into a corner. However, Moto Guzzi riders swear there is no adverse effect.

Certainly, the design had little effect on the machines in competition. In their second outing, Moto Guzzi won the Targa Florio, the round Sicily race, and kept on winning for thirty-six more years of factory-backed racing.

The original flat cylinder set-up with a low-slung, tubular, double-cradle frame served Moto Guzzi well. It was in production up until 1976. It did have its variations for racing, though. In 1924, race machines had four-valve heads. There were also 250 cc multi-cylinder, supercharged versions. In the mid-1930s, supercharged Moto Guzzis took most of the major race prizes. The year 1935 saw Moto Guzzi twins do a legendary Isle of Man TT double with Irishman Stanley Woods riding. Woods hacked away at a 47-second lead by Jimmy Guthrie on a Norton, and caused a sensation by foregoing his penultimate lap refuelling stop. Spectators waited in agony throughout the seventh and last lap. Woods came through in first place, four seconds ahead of Guthrie. He had smashed the lap record by 1 minute 7 seconds.

Moto Guzzi benefitted from the high post-war demand for the relatively cheap motorcycle. Indeed, there were more two-wheelers on the Italian roads than four-wheelers right up until the early 1960s. The star of Guzzi's output in the post-war years, however, was a true classic – the Falcone. Like the Daytona twin today, the 1950 500 cc (30 cu ins) single-cylinder Falcone was the ultimate development of the basic Guzzi single of 1921. The Falcone was produced until 1952, when the model was sub-divided into two – the Turismo and the original model renamed as the "Sport".

The Falcone retained the external flywheel and was nicknamed the "Bologna Bacon-Slicer". The long, flat engine means a longish wheelbase and therefore the Falcone performs better on straight and curvy roads rather than tight, twisting ones. One of the distinctive features of the Falcone is its sound; the elasticity of the engine gives it the distinctive hollow tone of the Guzzi exhaust – pulsing beats that make you think you can hear almost every explosion of the engine. Excellent low revving torque was accompanied by a top speed of 134 km/h (84 mph).

The Falcone was a dignified machine enjoyed by well-to-do enthusiasts, and its refinement typifies Italian post-war design at a time when cost-cutting did not enter into the equation. Indeed, in 1954, a Falcone Sport was nearly twice the cost of a Norton Dominator and £34 more expensive than a Vincent Black Shadow.

Moto Guzzi in the 1950s were able to invest in a lot of research and development. One piece of capital equipment which soon bore fruit was the windtunnel. The scientific use of the windtunnel meant the emergence of fairings on racing Moto Guzzis from 1953. One machine which benefitted

more than most was the amazing 500 cc (30 cu ins), eight-cylinder machine designed by Guilio Cesare Carcano, the head of the Guzzi race department, in 1954. The engine was built by Carcano and engineer Umberto Todero (who still works at Moto Guzzi today) during the winter of 1954-1955. The initial watercooled engine had two rows of four cylinders in a 90-degree V-configuration with eight carburettors and one common float chamber. On the last version, each carburettor had its own float chamber. Each bank of cylinders had double overhead cams. Amazingly, the resulting motorcycle weighed only 150 kg (330 lbs) – a modern lightweight Honda Fireblade weighs 181 kg (400 lbs).

Unfortunately, after a long period of development, the "Eight-Cylinder" was never really raced in anger. Like many other Italian manufacturers, Moto Guzzi opted out of racing in 1957. However, the bike did set an average 10 km speed record of 280 km/h (175 mph) in 1957. A record which did not fall until 1986.

Moto Guzzi's reason for pulling out of racing was financial. There were signs in the late 1950s that a recession was underway for motorcycle manufacturers. All the development by Carcano, Todero and others was shelved as sales plummetted with the resurgence of the small car. The company suffered badly and confined itself to small, lightweight machinery. The Carlo Guzzi engine, the flat-single, was removed from production, except for military and police orders. Carlo Guzzi died in 1964, and

soon after, a series of bad management decisions led to the company being forcibly administered by the state. It is worth noting that the Italian government provided a period of stability for the industry at a time when the British government was turning away from its motorcycle producers.

Carcano resigned during this period. Ironically, all his experience and development in the 1950s started to bear fruit commercially after his departure. A Carcano design for a big V-twin was produced as the 750 cc (45 cu ins) V-7 in

ABOVE: A 1952 Moto Guzzi Falcone Sport with its distinctive external flywheel.

1967. The market, starting to revive, was attuned, particularly in the States, to big machinery and the V-7 did quite well, securing vital military orders at the expense of designs by Ducati and Gilera. Developed by Lino Tonti, the V-7, became the 1971 Sport with its five-speed gearbox and stiff, double cradle frame. This design has been Moto Guzzi's stable output for the last twenty years and has included the legendary Le Mans series.

A notable exception in the era of the V-twin was the re-emergence of the Falcone flat-single in

1970. The Nuovo Falcone was not a success, but underlined the difficulties facing the company at the time. They needed to broaden their product range, but had limited resources; the Falcone line still existed for military and police orders so it was a viable option. Yet another case of the small motorcycle producer asking himself: "What can I make and hope to sell?"

At the present-day Moto Guzzi factory, the

BELOW: **A 1946 Gilera Saturno Sport, a big single with guts and gusto.**

abundance of old machining equipment underlines the difficulties of trying to make the sums balance while producing essentially hand-assembled motorcycles on a limited basis. The same old ghosts come back to haunt, and the problems with electrics and accessories will not go away. Guzzi have to be competitive on price and have to compromise on things like screw clamps and electrics just to contain costs.

The Italian problem, financially, has its roots in

an inherently inward-looking nature. For example, after many race victories around the world, Moto Guzzi has only recently got to grips with world markets. Only their single and V-twin really had a presence outside Italy. Their range of small, commuter models was for domestic consumption. Problems with supply of machinery, spares and service backup have dogged foreign dealers of all Italian marques right up until the 1980s. International racing success did not necessarily mean an international perspective or business attitude. Old Italian establishments were often family-run businesses, people who did not think on a large scale, and who were satisfied with making a beautiful bike, a masterpiece. Often, they would be content with selling a small number of models in their local area and shied away from mass-production, exportation and all its administrative and organizational problems.

Again, the numbers tell the tale. Moto Guzzi's total output in 1992 was 5,500 machines compared to Honda's 3.8 million. The Daytona superbike is to be limited to two production runs of 500. To mass-produce and cost-compete with the Japanese would involve a capital investment of many millions. Moto Guzzi are stuck in a difficult rut. If a factory is set up to make V-twins and it cannot afford to retool, V-twins is what it makes.

One of the oldest and most revered makes in Italy is Gilera. Like Moto Guzzi, they too have suffered from long periods of under-investment and stagnation. Now, however, they are a vibrant force

in motorcycling, not just in racing and design terms, but in financial terms too. The company, which was founded by Giuseppe Gilera in 1909, won many trials and long-distance road events throughout the 1920s and 1930s. The late 1930s saw a period of Grand Prix success and involvement in record-breaking. Their post-war road and racing bikes earned them great respect and profit, but they suffered through the 1960s more than most. The ailing company was bought by the Piaggio organization in 1969, and for the first time in Italian motorcycle production, a successful business with an understanding of mass-production efficiency was coupled with a marque which had a tradition and reputation. A long, clear look at the market showed a potential increase in the smaller, commuter end of the market. Also important was a return to successful competition.

Throughout the 1970s and 1980s, Gilera exploited the off-road trials scene and created a whole generation of small street-legal "enduro" lookalikes that sold well. The use of competition success and strong sales, rather than passion and pride, means that Gilera, in conjunction with Piaggio, is now one of the top five motorcycling producers in the world – all this without a significant loss of Italian style. Indeed, in 1985, Gilera brought out the Nuova Saturno – a 500 cc (30 cu ins) single-cylinder café racer for Japanese customers hungry for a machine which would evoke memories of the Italian heyday.

It is, however, for the original Gilera Saturno,

that the company is best known. It was the Moto Guzzi Falcone's main rival in the 1950s and a princely machine – the Italian equivalent of the BSA Gold Star. The 1946 Gilera Saturno initially straddled pre- and post-war technologies. Developed from the 1938 500 cc (30 cu ins) single, the "Otto Bullone", (the "Eight Bolt"), the Saturno had girder forks and unique parallelogram rear suspension. It came out initially as two models, the Turismo and the Sport. The Sport is capable of about 135 km/h (85 mph) with power output around 22 bhp at 5,000 rpm. The Saturno differed from the Eight Bolt in that it had overhead valves with the push-rod tunnels cast into the cylinder. It also featured a combined engine and gearbox "unit construction", instead of the separate, or "pre", units like many English bikes of the time. Its big 500 cc (30 cu ins) engine, which formed part of the frame, had a huge oil sump to aid cooling. All of these features made it a very tidy machine: it lacked a mass of messy external oil pipes and tanks.

The Saturno's classic status was gained by maturation. It was the basis of Gilera's 1950s output. The consequent simplicity and reliability of the design meant Gilera could exploit it to the full. Racing, touring and motocross versions followed. Bowing to fashion, the Saturno was later given telescopic forks, but they were not an improvement on the original girder forks.

The Saturno represents another strand of the complex weave that makes the Italian classic – patience. This means sticking with a formula that works when others may be clutching at the latest fashions in a desperate attempt to gain sales.

The Italian industry as a whole still continues to struggle against the Japanese in a shrinking market. Yet the Japanese are obsessed with capturing the qualities that they feel their machines lack. The Italian motorcycle has a mystique that Japanese mass-production has thus far failed to synthesize. Cliché or not, Italy's cultural history allows for a dualism that seems like a symptom of severe split personality to outsiders. It has had three momentous Empires shape its psyche: its distant history of the Roman Empire bequeaths a love of the sensual and decadent; its huge Christian tradition urges restraint and devotion; the great Renaissance brought an indulgent reverence for the aesthetic. So, in every aspect of Italian society there is a curious mix of the sacred and profane, the virtuous and the lazy. In Italy, artistic perfection can sit happily next to a "domane" attitude – do it tomorrow!

The Italian classic motorcycle's heritage comes shamelessly from the cult of the individual, from an unbalanced approach, from a glorious disrespect for economic good sense and an obsessive lust for perfection. In a world where vast project teams respond quickly and logically to ever-changing customer demands, the Italian classic now looks positively refreshing.

SCOOTER MANIA

The scooter brings with it diverse identities. Mostly it's remembered as the scooter of 1964, Mods on board, travelling down the road, an icon of public disorder. It is a memory of threatening over-customization, a statement of challenging excess. The scooter of 1960s Britain was a simple form of transport that was forced to join the rebel motorcycle on the wrong side of the rails. But while the two-wheeled highway led right through the centre of the swinging sixties, the scooter was about to take a premature side-turning to obscurity. How different from the grand plan it all was!

The scooter did not always belong to the Mods, it first belonged to Italy, to be exact post-war Italy. From 1945 to 1960, the Italian scooter eclipsed the traditional motorcycle. In Britain, in 1959, over half the 330,000 new two-wheeler registrations of that year were scooters. While the Mods and Rockers clashes of 1963 and 1964 may have been overhyped by the media, the scootermania of the 1950s was more than real. And this was no accidental phenomenon. Two large Italian industrial companies, Piaggio and Innocenti, orchestrated a manufacturing and marketing plan that literally shifted millions of their unique products, the Vespa and the Lambretta.

OPPOSITE: **This is the modern world! A Lambretta TV125 offers optimism and freedom to the "Baby Boomers".**

In 1945, Italy was in ruins. Daylight bombing by the Americans had destroyed the country's infrastructure. Most of the manufacturing areas had been blitzed; roads and railways had been blown up to halt the retreat of the Germans. The whole country had to be rebuilt. In 1946, Italy was a country going through what the Italians called "*La Reconstruzione*", the reconstruction period. All the great architects and designers of the day devoted themselves to public-service housing schemes. Italy had its industrial revolution in 1946, not in 1780. Despite the hardships, though, this was an extremely fertile period for business, with national optimism running high. This was a country desperately trying to throw off the mantle of facism, regain parlimentary democracy and, ultimately, modernize itself.

The Piaggio factory at Pontadera, near Milan, was a mass of rubble in 1945. Founded in 1884, Enrico Piaggio's heavy industrial operation had moved into aviation in 1915, making record-breaking aircraft engines in the 1930s and ending up making bombers for the Italian airforce during the war. As hostilities ceased, they were quickly forced to find a product for their idle workforce to make.

Supported financially by the Americans, the Italian government was offering grants to companies which could provide, amongst other things, basic transport. Motor car construction was too large a proposition at the time, so like many others, Piaggio decided to start a short-term project to make a cheap two-wheeler that could be operated by anyone and could navigate the pot-holed roads. The project still continues.

The company had been making 98 cc (6 cu ins) petrol engines which the Italian airforce used to drive airplane generators. The first Vespa appeared in 1946 with a 98 cc (6 cu ins) engine.

BELOW: **A national treasure – a papal blessing for the millionth Vespa.**

The Vespa was the most radical design for a two-wheeler ever seen. It renounced the whole notion of a motorcycle; the only feature it had in common seemed to be the two wheels.

It was designed by Corradino D'Ascanio, Italy's foremost helicopter designer. His complete lack of experience in motorcycle design meant that he approached the problem from first principles:

"I spent many sleepless nights trying to find the most basic and simple way I could to deal with these problems. Eventually, I sat down at the drawing-board and outlined the problem in this way. I arrived at a solution thus:

I started with the drawing of a person seated comfortably on a seat and I symmetrically arranged the man with two wheels. Under the seat I decided to completely cover the backwheel with a mud-guard. Finally, the front wheel was given a steering column. Immediately, a design had been born....'

A great deal of careful and subtle reinvention has gone on during the Vespa's history. This charmingly disingenuous D'Ascanio quote falls in with the generally pedalled version that D'Ascanio was trying to make a two-wheeled car and got it right first time. Actually his first design, the Paperino, named after the Italian version of Donald Duck, was a failure and only 100 were made. Piaggio sent him back to the drawing-board. Nevertheless, his second design, the Vespa – Italian for "wasp" – was unveiled in 1946 at the Turin Show to great acclaim.

Stephen Bayley, the design historian believes the Vespa is:

…genuinely one of the very, very great product designs. Two entirely different sources of inspiration make the Vespa into the very special machine it is. One is aesthetic, the other is technical. The aesthetic aspects of it are that it is a wonderfully wilful contrivance. It's an expression of pure sculptural form. It's a work of art, a small work of art in a way.

D'Ascanio was heavily influenced by his background in aerospace technology. Features like stub axles, the use of a stressed skin – monocoque construction – and aerodynamic details were derived straight from aerospace practice.

While the Vespa soon had many competitors, only one other design achieved the same status and sales: the Lambretta.

The Lambretta project was started by Ferdinando Innocenti almost at the same time as the Vespa. Like Piaggio, Innocenti's company was a big operation with a long history in heavy manufacturing and used existing technologies and American money to give them a head start in scooter production. Again, the scooter project was

RIGHT: A 1952 Douglas Vespa made under licence in Bristol.

only intended to be a temporary sideline.

The Lambretta was designed by a team headed by Pier Luigi Torre, under the close personal supervision of Ferdinando Innocenti. It got its name from the River Lambret which ran past the factory on the outskirts of Milan. It was another radical design, but different in many ways to the Vespa. Rather than being inspired by aircraft design and streamlining, the Lambretta grew out of Innocenti's expertise in steel tube applications. Visually, it was really more akin to the explicit functionalism of pre-war

LEFT: The cute little Lambretta A. The open design is regarded by many as the true spirit of Lambretta.

Bauhaus chairs. It had lots of chromium tubes and, uniquely, the early models up until the D did not have enclosed engines. Many enthusiasts argue that these were the last true Lambrettas. Because of its visibility, the engine's design was meticulously thought out both functionally and aesthetically. The ribbings on the casting were there to increase the feeling of compactness in the design. On the left side, the fan housing was designed as an attempt to produce images of turbines, a very modern concept at the time. Similarly, the heavily-dished wheels were very much like the racing car or airplane wheels of the period. From the outset, this machine had been designed to appeal to a mass market of consumers who would not necessarily like motorcycles, but who wanted a machine which was very futuristic. Rather than adopt a traditional sports image, it had much more of a science-fiction look, at a time when images of Dan Dare and the Mekon travelling around on magic machines that floated across the ground were extremely potent.

The Vespa and the Lambretta remobilized Italy. Demand outpaced supply. Despite the wide availability of cheap labour, raw material costs were high. Scooters cost less than cars but were not very cheap. Nevertheless, hundreds of thousands of Italians made great sacrifices just to have one. The Vespa and Lambretta were irresistible. Just like Marcello Uzoli's Olivetti typewriter and Achille Castiglione's cappucino machines, they were designed to be stylish in a world of post-war drudgery. They delivered precisely what they promised — clean, reliable and smart transport – and so became symbols of national hope and optimism.

From 1950-51 there was an increase of 50 per cent in road traffic in Italy. Of the vehicles on the road, 80 per cent were scooters. Another key to their success was that both the Lambretta and Vespa were designed to be immediately usable by anyone. You just got on and drove off. These were not meant to be high-speed sports machines but, rather, as the Lambretta instruction booklet of the time said: "a utility, practical, comfortable, restful, transportation means".

As Piaggio and Innocenti's products were designed to be totally unlike motorcycles of the day, they carried none of the negative associations. The public's perception of motorbikes was of complex machinery which dripped, leaked and exploded at random. In a culture where personal vanity is a high priority, such a device would not have been popular amongst people who liked to have creases in their trousers and to wear silk even when they go to work. The Vespa's leg guards and all-enclosing body work were not merely a concession to aircraft and automobile design, they were also a clear recognition of customer needs.

Underpinning the Vespa's and Lambretta's success as aesthetic and functional objects was the fact that they were two solid pieces of engineering made by two essentially modern companies. In this respect, Piaggio and Innocenti were not typical of the indigenous motorcycle industry. (For example, Innocenti's 7,000 strong workforce had many

fringe benefits including sports and health facilities, a swimming pool, an advice centre and scholarships for employees' children. Honda, in Japan, was not the first to realize the importance of a loyal workforce.) Up until the Second World War, motorcycle manufacturers offered small production runs of handbuilt machines. Piaggio and Innocenti brought big business to Italian two-wheeler production. Both were familiar with conveyor-belt, mass-production techniques. They installed up-to-the-minute equipment. Right from the start they had

ABC SKOOTAMOTA

Part of the motorcyclist's hatred for scooters stems from an earlier period of scootermania. Although it was confined mostly to one summer, Britain went wild for scooters in 1919. Again, this was a function of post-war liberation. Designs like the ABC Skootamota, the Unibus and the Autoped hit the headlines; the Skootamota made it into Selfridge's window and there was a great deal of press coverage of the phenomenon. The reality of this craze was considerably less impressive; few machines were actually built and sold. However, the notion of the running board, central to scooter design, originated at this time. The 155 cc (9 cu ins) ABC Skootamota was aimed at women, so the step-through frame mirrored that of the lady's bicycle. It was also low-powered. But the technology of the time could not create a sufficiently strong structure that would resist torsional stress, so the machines were difficult to handle. Such machines were seen by "purists" as playthings, an adjunct to mainstream motorcycles. The bigotry persisted even if the scooters did not.

volume production and relatively low costs.

The Vespa and the Lambretta ended up looking virtually identical, but their origins were quite different. Piaggio's expertise was in pressed steel construction. The Vespa's body is made from pressed steel sections spot-welded together to form one stress-bearing shell – a monocoque. All other components are bolted to that shell. The Vespa is a snail, an invertebrate. The Lambretta, however, has a spine. Innocenti's background in steel tubing manufacture meant that the Lambretta evolved with a central load-bearing tube, to which were attached footboards, legshields and the engine. Unlike the Vespa, the Lambretta's running board and side panels have no stiffening function.

The Vespa had an elegantly designed engine.

The motor and gearbox sat side-by-side, the whole thing cooled by a fan. This compact unit was directly connected to the rear wheel and moved up and down as part of the suspension system. This minimized transmission lash — a sort of lurching to and fro — common with chain drive, and also minimized friction loss. This made the Vespa engine one of the most efficient two-stroke power units ever developed. Constant improvement and expansion, rather than redesign, led to the arrival of the now classic 150 cc (9 cu ins) Vespa GS range.

While the Lambretta was no less unique, it started with shaft drive and no rear suspension and then went through a number of design changes before settling on a sprung, combined engine and rear-wheel unit with chain drive. This new engine unit powered the classic TV175 and the late 1960s slimline models like the SX.

Both companies tried to outpace each other by bringing in more and more powerful models. Soon the 55 km/h (35 mph) scooter could do over 110 km/h (70 mph). Lambretta won the power battle, but they had to concede the popularity of the enclosed look. That popularity was a clear indication of the public's psychological linking of the scooter to the car. There was no functional need to cover up the "working" parts of the Lambretta, as there was never any risk or indeed any damage caused. The change was purely aesthetic. In fact, Lambretta virtually held a public referendum on this change. The 1952 125 cc (7 cu ins) Model D, which was basically the original design, was accompanied by

BELOW: This cut-away drawing of a Lambretta Slimstyle shows the elegance and economy of design. The snaking single tube can be seen running from the handlebars down, along the floor, up and back above the engine. The integral rear wheel and engine can also be seen with its enclosed chaindrive.

the LD, its fully-clothed sister. The public made their feelings perfectly clear. Innocenti stopped producing open models in 1958.

From the point of view of design, the macho motorcycling diehards were appalled by scooters. They claimed the engine over the back wheel made the machines unstable. There was little truth in the claim and in fact the small wheels improved braking. Yet, in 1950s Britain, dyed-in-the-wool motorcycle dealers refused to stock or repair the Lambretta and Vespa. Motorcycle manufacturers, however, were forced to take the threat seriously as scooter sales rocketed, boosted by another new fad — hire purchase. Belatedly, the other manufacturers got in on the act, but largely it was a disaster story. The Italian motor scooter had been conceived as a complete

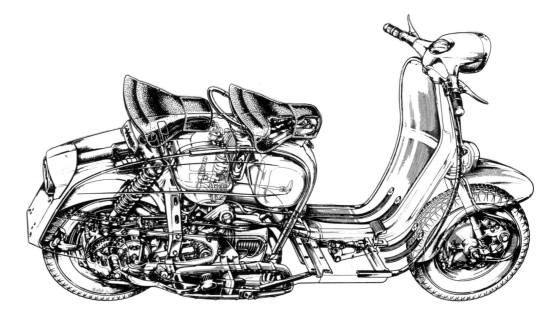

product. It was not simply a proprietary engine lashed to the rear wheel by a chain, with quirky body shape to boot. It was designed from scratch. What the others could not master was the blend of lightness and sophistication of design with strong engineering reliability. The British industry produced scooters which reflected its heavy engineering tradition. They tended to be overweight and underpowered by proprietary Villers two-stroke engines. The DKR Dove was one such machine. The BSA Sunbeam was another. The Sunbeam was exactly what scooters should not have been; it was a lash-up job and the bodywork hid the terrible mess from the public's eye. It was a clear example of the fact that the Vespa and Lambretta's British imitators did not truly understand the essence of the machine. They simply were not "with it".

The establishment was blind to the modern world and the Vespa and Lambretta were expressions of the need for change. British scooters were hastily thrown-together efforts from an old world order. (A good seller, though, was the made-in-Britain "Douglas Vespa" under licence from Piaggio.) The only real competition came from Germany – the 200 cc (12 cu ins) Zundapp Bella and 195 cc (12 cu ins) electric start TWN Contessa were attempts at integrated design and sold well. The Heinkel Tourist was well made and popular, if a bit bulky; it could do an easy 95 km/h (60 mph). But Vespa and Lambretta had a head start on everyone, even strong domestic designs like the Rumi Formichino, and could close the performance gaps quickly. By the

The Scintillating **BSA SUNBEAM**

early 1950s, the Italian style machine was rolling on a new wave of modernism throughout Europe. The streamlined jet set were going places. In the process of mobilizing Italy, the Vespa and the Lambretta had mobilized the youth of the world.

But scootering was *engineered* to be more than a form of transportation. It became a major social pastime. The manufacturers went to great efforts to encourage scooterists to join their clubs. The Lambretta Club of Great Britain brought out its own magazine, *The Jet Set*. Rallies, runs, games and even beauty contests were staged, all extending the exciting continental image purveyed in Scooter advertizing.

The two rivals presented their machines in very similar ways. Around them they wrapped images which were the antithesis of wartime life – freedom, love, burgeoning youth, sex, fun, scooters for the young and the young at heart. Advertizing was handled by mainstream publications – *The Financial Times*, *Équipe*, *Life*, *Esquire*, *National Geographic*. As a result, non-motorcyclists flocked to the scooter.

The carefree, idealized world of the scooter proclaimed the scooter as a new product, distancing it ideologically even further from the old macho motorcycle. One huge difference was that scooter manufacturers targetted women as potential customers. In the adverts, *women* were seen shopping and at leisure driving these machines. It was glamorous for women to be seen driving one, with the obligatory Hermes scarf around their head to

OPPOSITE: **The advertising caught the right mood, but the mechanics failed to deliver the dream. Only a handful of BSA Sunbeams were sold worldwide.**

RIGHT: **A Lambretta ad from 1964 for the Li 125-150 cc "Slimstyle" range.**

protect their hairstyle. Film stars like Raquel Welch and Ursula Andress were seen on Vespas. Angie Dickinson and Kate O'Mara went whizzing away from Cinecittà on them. Competition grew between the two companies to see who could get their machine in a feature film, the most notable success being the Vespa carrying Audrey Hepburn and Gregory Peck in *Roman Holiday*. In New York, Lambrettas were sold in exclusive fashion shops.

However, the scooter's relationship with women was often contradictory. While women were encouraged to take control of these machines themselves, the women were still used as an

LEFT: The ultimate incarnation of the Vespa dream: St Tropez, a girl in a little dress, a boy in dark chinos, polo shirt and sunglasses.

adornment. Vespa calenders of the 1950s and 1960s show scantily-clad models in a variety of international locations sprawled over their machines. The archetypal scooter image must surely be the young continental male in a lambswool sweater driving his Vespa, while his dutiful girlfriend sits side-saddle behind him popping grapes into his mouth: sell to the women on the easy-to-use values, sell to the men using good old sex.

The two companies also pushed the customer to live the jet-set image of their PR films. The idea of travelling around sunny Europe on these things was fundamental to the scooters' modern "see-the-world" image. They carried quite a lot of luggage, and there was a space for a rack on the back and front. You could even have luggage in the gap in the step-through frame. However, some PR films inadvertently show a less glamorous image. In *Travel Far and Wide* (Innocenti 1954), a long line of Lambrettas cross a rainy Alpine pass. Perhaps this was nearer the truth. Piaggio and Innocenti did more than create a stylish product and present it stylishly. The packaging went further. They ensured scootering lived up to its problem-free, easy-to-use image. An international network of dealers and workshops were set up; it was not necessary to get your hands dirty with a scooter.

At the time, motorcyclists relished the prospect of doing the necessary weekly maintenance and repairs on their machines. Scooterists, on the other hand, were not expected to endure the same incessant tinkering as the addicted enthusiasts.

The wheels, being small, meant that it was possible to carry a spare. This was, of course, unheard of on a solo motorcycle. The fact that the wheels at the front and the back of a scooter were identical, meant that if you got a puncture you simply changed the wheel – just like a car. During the 1950s, Innocenti's service network also boasted

BELOW: The basic manufacturer's accessories pre-echo some of the later Mod styles.

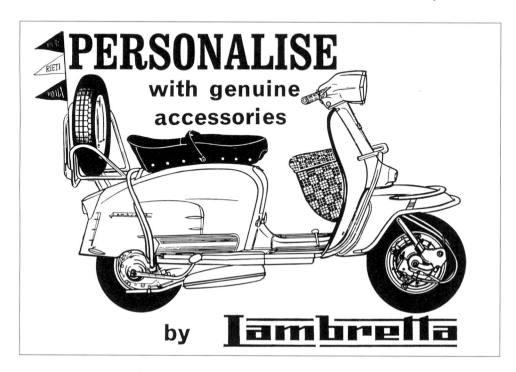

a guaranteed engine replacement exchange service so that if a Lambretta went wrong, the whole power unit was removed and sent back to the factory, while it was replaced on the spot by a reconditioned one. The scooter was a much more convenient, user-friendly machine all round because of these "designed-in" attributes.

As scooter engines got bigger, great pains were taken to display the supposedly feminine machines' masculine prowess by defeating the hardest obstacles. The factories had mad-cap stunt teams. Numerous speed records were undertaken. A 1951 Lambretta in full fairing broke the flying kilometre record for its class with a speed of 200 km/h (125mph). Scooters took part in the 960 kilometre (600-mile) Milan–Taranto race, the 24 hour Bol D'Or races and even held their own Isle of Man TT. Soon the public were aping the manufacturers' stunts, doing their best to break these seemingly unbreakable machines. In Britain, they held a rally which took them to the summit of Ben Nevis and back.

Customization and accessorization were also becoming popular by the late 1950s and the manufacturers, ever keen to oblige, offered a large range of clip-on extras. The threatening, heavily-customized scooters of the early 1960s grew out of this innocent trend. Eddy Grimstead, an East-London dealer, turned the trend into an art form by offering paint schemes to the owner's design. The Royal College of Art magazine, *ARK*, hailed him as an unconscious prophet of the Pop Art movement!

LEFT: 1966 – the year, as opposed to the number of lights.

The relationship of the scooter to the Mods, however, is much more complex than paint jobs, whip aeriels or fox's tails. Inspired by Marcello Mastroianni in *La Dolce Vita* and the gangs in *West Side Story*, a small group of London boys began, in the late 1950s, to ape Continental and American summer styles. The love of the modern gave them their name. Smartness was essential, especially as the previous youth movement, the Rockers, were greasy and slovenly. Being up-to-the-minute meant being into anything Italian – haircuts, suits and frothy coffee. And the Mods, like any other youth movement in the early 1960s, had to get around.

OPPOSITE: Functional Fashion - the parka and the running board are keeping this Mod's suit and feet nice and dry, thank you.

They had to be seen at cafés, clubs and dances. Mostly they travelled by public transport. A few adopted the scooter because it was clean, it kept their Zoot suits pristine and, more than anything, it symbolized a modern world.

The Mod association with the scooter, although initially positive, turned sour as a result of the disturbances in British south-coast resorts in 1963 and 1964. The crude characterization of these amorphous events as "Mods vs Rockers" and thus "Scooters vs Motorbikes" was largely created by the press. In reality, the clashes tended to be an extension of typical Bank Holiday weekend excess. The large influx to the coast from London and the surrounding area was swelled by a new class of socially-mobile youth. There was trouble but it was more to do with London vs the south coast than Mod vs Rocker. The reported mayhem was, at worst, two stabbings at Margate in 1964, but the polarisation became a self-fulfilling prophecy.

The motorcyclists' disdain for the engineering principles of the scooter was mapped elegantly onto the Mod-Rocker music and style divide. Despite its minimal involvement, the scooter achieved cult and, thus, lowbrow status.

Ironically, the real nail in the scooter's coffin was a much less anti-establishment source – the Mini. This provided cheap transport for the masses, but this time with four seats and a roof. It had all the attributes of modern style – little wheels, smoothed-off edges, bright fancy colours. Ironically, Innocenti started making the Mini under licence in Italy. When the company got into financial trouble in 1973, the terms of the Mini deal meant that British Leyland took over the company. They saw the Lambretta as a gimmick and stopped production. The establishment pulled the plug, but the Mods got the blame anyway.

The Vespa fared little better and sales declined from the mid-1960s onward. However, sales later stabilized and Piaggio still continue to produce the Vespa in competition with the Japanese. The need for a cheap runabout in the age of the car is limited, but it suits the Italian urban landscape of tight mediaeval streets. The Lambretta is still made under licence in India. It continues to mobilize developing nations.

The scooter's success was the result of the first proper combination of big-business mentality, engineering excellence and the Italian passion for design. It was also one of the first mass-marketed products and probably the first European product to be "packaged". It created its own era and went on to outlive it. It created a new verb in the Italian language, "*vespizzarre*" – to travel by scooter. The scooter has not died; it exists now as a category of transport, as a class of object. It has risen above itself.

The Vespa and Lambretta were objects finely tuned to their time. If they had one, their biggest tragic flaw was that they were fashion objects and as such they were doomed to go out of fashion. Now, however, they are simply "classic".

FLIGHT TO MUNICH

The story of German motor-cycling is not dissimilar to that of the United States. From the pioneer days there grew a vibrant industry with many manufacturers, producing many classic designs. However, the general output of roadgoing designs has been fairly conservative. There the similarity with the United States ends. Today there are only two German motor-cycle manufacturers who are still in business. One of the extant marques is BMW; everyone knows them, if only for their cars. The other is MuZ, formerly MZ, – less well known for their small, cheap two-strokes. A BMW motorcycle is the solid, dependable, stately, upmarket machine for the respectable rider. MZ, recently available from behind the Iron Curtain, has long been dull, downmarket commuter fodder. From these two sources stems the unfortunate label of "boring" that German motorcycles have acquired.

At first it seems that what Germany has failed to offer the motorcyclist is a wild, fire-

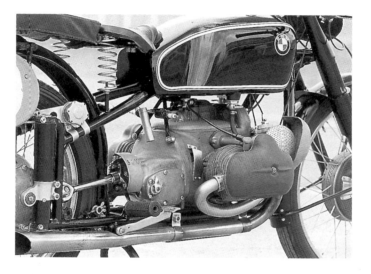

ABOVE: A beautiful, super-charged 1939 BMW 500 cc Type 255 racer.

OPPOSITE: Look out behind you! A Norton outfit about to be overhauled in the TT by the all-powerful BMW teams.

breathing street racer. There is no equivalent in the history of German motorcycling of the BSA Gold Star, the Ducati 900SS or the Kawasaki Z1. But then neither is there a very recent American equivalent. Yet American motor-cycles, even in their present state, can by no means be described as boring; what they have in common with the street racer is menace. German machinery is not menac-ing; it does not "let go". If it has a threatening quality, it lies not in one machine, but in the ceaseless production of high-quality engi-neering, model after model. The reason that German motorcycling has not tried to churn out "crotch rockets" is because it is founded on very different psychological principles.

In German thinking everything has to be in its proper place, doing its proper job. Even the German language follows, or maybe leads, this atti-tude. There is no flexibility, no variation. German grammar is complex but exact and the basic German character believes in a right and a wrong way. The desire to ride wild and fast is thus seen largely as an error. The solution is not to provide machinery to satisfy this urge, but to encourage sensible riding. This is the German way and other countries can do as they please.

The Germans tend to view production motor-cycling as largely about travel and leisure, reliability and innovative design. They are less interested in the idea of being the outsider. Great motorcycle design has always had the erratic ability to synthe-size an essentially anti-social urge and transform it into a barely-restrained mechanical package. German motorcycle design, up until now, has not

BELOW: A two-speed, 4 hp NSU having just completed a trans-America crossing in 1910 – 3,734 miles in 28 days and 2 hours.

tried to satisfy that small, but persistent, craving.

This is surprising, because Germany is a country which knows all the glory and pain of motorcycle production and racing. While its long lineage of manufacturers have shown an inclination to middle-ground production for the masses, Germany has many extreme examples of motor-cycling endeavour. The country's heritage of innov-ative and record-breaking motorcycles ranges from the massive 1800 cc (110 cu ins), 160 bhp Munch Titan to the World Championship dominating 50 cc (3 cu ins) Kreidler, but it is hallmarked by a dedication to the highest principles of engineering. The competitive urge is strong in the German character, but it must be precisely and clinically controlled. From the German point of view, the American obsession with power, the Italian passion, the British gung-ho attitude are all considered "emotional" responses which should be eliminated. The Germans do not take as many chances with design, because that often means Glory or Bust and the German way cannot tolerate such imprecision. The revered elements of German design are ultra-high quality, a redoubtable scientific approach and a distinguished history in aero-engineering. And, of course, it should not be forgotten that the first four-stroke cycle engine was created by a German Nikolaus August Otto, in 1876. German motor-cycling has blue blood.

For example, the sadly now extinct company, NSU, was a manufacturer of high-quality standard machines from the pioneer days – they took part in

the first Isle of Man TT in 1907. However, they are remembered for their Rennmax and Rennfox racing machines which dominated Grand Prix racing in the 1950s. At that time, NSU was a major competitor in the world of motorcycle racing; they established new precedents in scientific research and development and professionalism. On the roads, however,

BELOW: On the right a 250 cc NSU Supermax single, with its little brother, the 125 cc Superfox.

they are known for a completely different reason. When other manufacturers would have tried to bring out a rubber-burning road version of their race machines, the top-of-the-range NSU roadster, the 1956 Supermax, was an 18 bhp, 118 km/h (74 mph) general-purpose machine. All the factory's expertise had gone into the engineering of the

LEFT: **50 cc NSU Quickly moped.**

neered NSU Quickly moped. The 50 cc (3 cu ins) two-stroke was little more than a powered bicycle, but it remains one of the most successful commuter machines ever sold. While it is now overshadowed by more ubiquitous Japanese machines, over a million NSU Quicklys and variants were sold all over Europe from 1953 to 1962.

NSU's dedication to quality was matched by their rigorously scientific approach to racing. Their first attempt at Grand Prix level was with their 1951, in-line, four-cylinder 500 cc (30 cu ins) machine designed by Albert Roder. Influenced by contemporary Gileras, it raced well that season in national events. However, the management decided that they ought to compete in the 125 cc (7 cu ins) and 250 cc (15 cu ins) categories and the 500 cc (300 cu ins) technology was used to create a four-stroke 125 cc (7 cu ins) single, the R11 Rennfox. This machine boasted many exciting features, including a pressed-steel frame. Technically more exciting was the 1952 four-stroke, 250 cc (15 cu ins), twin-cylinder R22 Rennmax.

At the time, Moto Guzzi dominated the 250 cc (15 cu ins) class with their lightweight flat single-cylinder four-stroke. The Rennmax, designed by Dr Walter Froede, benefitted from the increased engine revs possible in its smaller-pistoned, twin-cylinder engine. Throughout the 1952 World Championship it was at the heels of the Guzzis. A much improved 1953 Rennmax, with small fairing, new pressed-steel frame and higher compression pistons, was put in the hands of newcomer Werner

machine. Its quality of finish was stunning, the petrol cap a work of art, the paintwork a deep mirror-like black. In quality alone it is a great classic. Nevertheless, the design was entirely out of touch with public needs and put the company into financial trouble. The Supermax was just too good for its market.

But it is not the Supermax for which NSU are best known. Ironically, NSU were kept afloat by their brilliantly conceived and exquisitely engi-

Haas. Out of nowhere, Haas became the first German to win a World Championship; and more than that, he won two – the 250 cc (15 cu ins) on the Rennmax and the 125 cc (7 cu ins) on the new, double-overhead cam Rennfox.

While these heady events were unfolding, Froede was busy making what was one of the first serious studies of the physics of a racing motorcycle engine. Using a separate engine to power a partially disassembled Rennfox engine, he steadily built the engine back up and measured the extra force required to turn it at each stage. He also experimented with alterations to the flow of the gases within the engine. Armed with advanced knowledge of internal frictions and efficient combustion, he redesigned the Rennmax engine and upped its power output from 32 bhp at 10,000 rpm to 39 bhp at 11,500 rpm. At the same time, the 1954 machine was lighter and sported a windtunnel-designed fairing. The competition, Moto Guzzi, also employed their new windtunnel to good effect. Technology on the race track was there to stay.

In 1954, a team of four Rennmaxes, led by Werner Haas, took the first four places in the 250 cc (15 cu ins) French GP, the first four places in the Lightweight Isle of Man TT, the first two places in the Ulster GP, the first three in the Dutch TT, the first two in the German GP, and first place in the Swiss GP, often at speeds greater than those of the winning machines in the bigger 350 cc (21 cu ins) class. Consequently, the 250 cc (15 cu ins) Rennmax

was bored out to 288 cc (17 cu ins) and took part in a handful of national events. Not surprisingly, it started to approach the speeds of the 500 cc (30 cu ins) class. The scene was set for a NSU 350 cc (21 cu ins) World Championship attempt the following year. Meanwhile, the 125 cc (7 cu ins) Rennfoxes, led by another new find, twenty-four-year-old Austrian Rupert Hollous, won the Isle of Man TT, took the first four places in the Ulster GP, the first two places in the Dutch TT, and the first two places in the German GP. Haas and Hollous were World Champions and the NSU dream looked like going on forever. Then, tragically, Hollous was killed in practice at the Monza GP. NSU withdrew all their riders as a mark of respect.

BELOW: A 1950s NSU Rennmax racer.

This love of the highest possible quality does not mean that German machines have always been exiled to a small area of expensive machinery production. There was a period when German machinery sold almost too well. In fact, the importation of German motorcycles into the UK had, by

ABOVE: The ubiquitous "Deek" – the RT125.

RIGHT: Simple, elegant evolution – the BMW R32, R100R and R1100RS.

They also withdrew from the following and final Grand Prix in Spain.

Riding on such a crest of publicity, which testified to the power and reliability of their machinery, one would have expected NSU to overcome this tragedy – at the time they were also doing well in trials and breaking numerous world speed records. But, in effect, Hollous' death was the catalyst for a management decision to pull out entirely from road racing. Grand Prix racing had been made pedestrian by NSU's complete domination, the press haranging them for being boring! Sadly, NSU stopped producing two-wheelers in 1965.

1939, become so great that the British, true to Prime Minister Chamberlain's style of appeasement, tried to enter into a price-fixing deal with the Germans. Exports of German machines were running at 33,679 for 1939, five times the amount of a decade previously; in an attempt at domination in

every sphere, Nazi Germany was dumping a great number of low-priced goods onto world markets. In the same period, British manufacturers were hitting trade barriers and exports had fallen to 19,000. However, the war put paid to that particular dilemma and Britain got its own back in motorcycling terms for a while. One of the main German victims was DKW.

DKW sat alongside NSUs in the world's showrooms of the 1930s. They started in 1920 with clip-on engines and progressed through the 1920s with pressed steel designs and small commuter machines. DKW two-strokes were a powerful force on 1930s race tracks and won the lightweight Isle of Man TT in 1938. Later, war reparations meant that the company's technology was given to the Allies, most notably the RT125. Remodelled as the BSA Bantam, the Harley-Davidson Hummer and numerous other reincarnations, the design made a lot of people outside Germany a lot of money. It was also later copied by Yamaha. The 1950s racing DKW two-strokes pioneered the use of expansion chambers and were innovative designs for the time.

Indeed, it is on the racetrack that German motorcycling aggression has, perhaps quite properly, been fully vented. The tiny Kreidler is a true classic and a testimony to rigorous persistence and love of exactitude. Kreidlers were the greatest 50 cc (3 cu ins) world championship machines of all time — from 1971 to 1983 Kreidler won seven world championships. Dr Alfred Kreidler got into motorcycle manufacture, like so many others, as part of the post-Second World War boom in cheap transport. In 1951, he made an ultra-reliable 50cc (3 cu ins) moped which soon became the number one choice for youngsters in Germany. By 1958, racing versions were being put onto the tracks by private racers. When the World Championship was formed in 1962, the factory put all its efforts into creating a machine which would give the Japanese a run for their money. The tiny German machine boasted a 49.9 cc (3 cu ins) two-stroke, rotary-valved engine with chrome-lined cylinder, twin Bing carburettors, and a twelve-speed gearbox! The frame was made of lightweight tubing, with Earles front forks, and shrouded in a windtunnel-evolved fairing. The whole thing weighed a mere 537 kg (118 lbs).

Kreidler won the first two Grand Prix of the season, but the small factory could not hold off the Suzuki which eventually won the title. This was the story again the following year and Kreidler pulled out of the championship after the 1965 season. But changes in the regulations, limiting the class to one cylinder and six gears, brought them back into competition in 1969. The old machines did not fare well in the first two seasons, but a new machine for 1971 did the trick. A revised, now watercooled engine and changed frame design meant that Kreidler took the title with Jan de Vries on board. Constant development of the tiny engine meant that it was hardly beaten throughout the 1970s until 1983, when the class was abandoned by the FIM.

Neither has Germany been short of enterprising individuals. Helmut Fath was an amazing character, who after surviving a horrendous sidecar crash in 1961, came back to win the 1968 World Championship with an in-line, four-stroke, four-cylinder, fuel-injected engine which he had made himself in his own home! He also supplied sidecar outfits to other racers. After a further injury, he became a celebrated two-stroke tuner and designed and made a flat four-cylinder, two-stroke engine which seriously challenged in the World Sidecar Championship, and would have been a serious 500 cc (30 cu ins) solo contender but for problems with the host machine's frame.

The "biggest bore" accolade, however, is mostly given to poor old BMW. What they provide for the discerning palate, however, is something a little more intriguing. You can get on a big BMW twin and stay at over 112 km/h (70 mph) all week long. Other machines would pack up or numb you with vibration. Is that boring or just good engineering? They last forever, and German reserve and gentlemanly manners are characteristics of their owners. Is that to be scoffed at?

The early machines tended to be built for long-distance cruising. Indeed, since they were ideal for Hitler's new autobahns, BMW grew massively in the 1930s, parallel to the expansion of Nazi Germany in that period. This aspect of the machines means they are ideal today for Euro-touring, but in the world motorcycle culture of the 1930s, dominated as it was by English style and

ABOVE: **A Fath Four in action, in1968.**

OPPOSITE: **The watch-like, miniature-marvel Kreidler.**

taste, they were unable to attract anything other than very sensible chaps in flat caps. It is the fellows with the mad glint in their eye who really inform wider opinion and affect sales. The company itself has had little desire to shrug off its unexciting image, motorcycles only occasionally being its core business.

In the pioneer era, one of BMW's predecessors – BFW (Bayerische Flugzeugwerke) – made very good aircraft engines. So good that Baron von Richthofen had his whole First World War fighter squadron kitted out with them. In 1917, BFW merged with another aviation company run by Gustav Otto, the son of the inventor of the four-stroke engine. The result was Bayerische Motoren Werke AG – BMW – the Bavarian Engine Works.

Then things fell apart. The Treaty of

Versailles, which, amongst other things, regulated the industrial output of the defeated Germany, brought a halt to BMW's production. But the young designers of BMW were all-consummed by aeronautics and continued to work in secret. Chief designer Max Friz finished his outstanding 300 hp six-cylinder engine in 1919; in a BFW biplane it set a new altitude record of over 11,665 m (32,000 ft). But the ambitious boys were discovered and had everything consfiscated by the Allies.

Like every other hamstrung company in Germany at the time, they scrabbled about for things to make that would keep them in business. Only four years later, BMW unveiled a Max Friz-designed motorcycle, the R32, which was the sensation of the 1923 Paris Show. Friz's classic BMW design is still being produced today.

However, Friz hated having to work on motorcycles. Really, he felt, it was beneath him. His love of aircraft design perhaps made him over-compensate for his loss by making a machine of outstandingly high quality for the time. The engine was a 493 cc (29 cu ins) flat twin. In this format, the two cylinders are set at 180 degrees to each other, thus cancelling out the forces generated as each piston is thrown outwards from the centre. The result is a very smooth, low-vibration engine. Friz mounted the engine transversely in the frame, so that the two cylinders stuck out both sides of the machine, in front of the rider's feet. Great for cold, Bavarian winters!

Friz also set in place the other two elements of the BMW Holy Trinity – a strong, stiff frame and, more importantly, shaft drive. When other motorcycles of the period were still struggling with rudimentary chain and belt drives, Friz equipped his BMW with a transmission that was clean and reliable.

To the motorcyclist of the 1920s, the R32 must have been a strange and beguiling beast. Unlike the general herd, the BMW engine seemed to be a solidly sculpted alloy block. Everything, like oilways, gearbox and timing were secreted in it. The aerodynamic background of its designer must have been obvious.

So, too, was the identity of a machine which had clearly influenced Friz. Designed by aero-engine designer, Granville Bradshaw, the 1920 ABC predates many of the BMW's features. It was very light, with everything made to aircraft standards. In addition to the transversely mounted, flat twin-cylinder, 400 cc (24 cu ins) engine, the motorcycle had a car-type clutch, car-type four-speed gearbox, front and rear suspension, internal expanding brakes and electric lighting. The elegance of the flat-twin engine design, however, did not translate in the first BMW, at any rate, into firepower. It was from the start a low-revving slogger with a top speed of just over 80 km/h (50 mph).

Soon after the R32's public debut, Max Friz returned to his real job of designing aero engines and with him went any notion of disinterest. A very keen young engineer, Rudolph Schleicher, took over. He produced a substantially uprated version, the R37, which featured overhead valve gear. The new engine revved harder and had twice the power – 16 bhp at 4,000 rpm. Far from pedestrian, the R37 won scores of road-racing competitions and the 1925 German Grand Prix. Schleicher, no armchair designer, also took his R37 to the International Six Days Trial in Britain and won a Gold Medal. Ernst Henne achieved further fame for BMW with a motorcycle speed record of 220.13 km/h (137.58 mph) in 1929.

Under Schleicher's guidance, BMW motorcycles progressed well technically through the

BELOW: **A 1950s BMW R69.**

MUNCH-MAMMOTH AND TITAN

The Munch-Mammoth is the story of Friedl Munch who put an 998 cc (60 cu ins) NSU four-cylinder car engine into a copy of a Norton Featherbed frame. His first prototype attracted Floyd Cylmer, an American publisher who owned the "Indian" name. Around 100 Mammoths were made and sold. Munch also made a prototype 1400 cc (85 cu ins), 125 bhp machine called the Daytona, in 1970, which was so powerful it shredded tyres. In 1986, Munch was commissioned to produce the Titan, an 1800 cc (109 cu ins), 160 hp supercharged monster, for a wealthy Californian. Not very boring!

1920s, but as a company, BMW moved into car production, so corporate attention was split three ways between cars, planes and motorcycles. This huge expansion meant a huge burden of debt just at a time when economic anarchy was about to visit Germany. Ironically, it was the company's diversity of output which allowed some quick shuffling of resources and kept the business going.

Aero engines sold well abroad and car production technology was used in motorcycle production. The result was that BMW brought out the world's first pressed-steel-frame motorcycles in 1929, the 745 cc (45 cu ins) R11, and the higher-revving 734 cc (44 cu ins) R16. BMW also resorted to tactics which have kept many motorcycle manufacturers afloat in the worst times. They brought out a small commuter machine – the pressed-steel-framed, 200 cc (12 cu ins) single-cylinder R2. Its bigger brother, the 398 cc (24 cu ins) R4, sold in volume to the German Army.

BMW expanded massively in the 1930s. They brought out the 745 cc (45 cu ins) R12 in 1935. Gone was the usual trailing-link front suspension, to be replaced with the first hydraulically-damped telescopic forks ever seen on a motorcycle. Also of note was the R17, a sports model with a power output of 33 bhp.

BMW displayed an interest in competition that bordered on keenness in the pre-war period, and they did quite well. Henne traded world speed records with the English and Italians and his super-charged 500 cc (30 cu ins) BMW hit 277 km/h (173 mph) in 1937, a record which stood until 1951. Best of all, Georg Meier and Jock West took a great first/second in the Isle of Man Senior TT in 1939. Hardly world domination stuff though, at a time when the Hitler government saw motorcycle sport as a showcase for superior German technology and were funding it accordingly.

The slow haul out of wartime devastation brought only steady improvement to the flat twins and singles. Radical innovation was not a hallmark of BMW in the 1950s. The real BMW classics of that time were the R50 and the R69. They featured Earles forks and new rear suspension, the drive shaft being accomodated in the right leg of the new swinging arm. The rear shock-absorbers were mounted low on the rear of the main loop frame

ABOVE: Georg Meier on his 1939 TT-winning BMW Rennsport.

and attached at the bottom of the shroud. This made the whole structure very rigid.

The whole approach of the factory, which the public clearly perceived, in the 1950s was inherent in these two machines: high-quality engineering, clean looks, luxurious performance at high speeds, excellent sidecar applicability and, above all, solid reliability. But, hang on! This was the era of the café racer! The BMW's broad gearing and engine speed clutch made it a non-starter in the traffic-lights Grand Prix. The Earles forks could cope with long slow curves, but on England's twisting country lanes they were liable to pitch you off.

The kids did not want it. It was an old man's bike!

The company's dull image also stems from a general lack of success on the post-war race circuit. The Munich-based factory was present and often acquitted itself very well in solo events throughout the 1950s and 1960s, yet very rarely did a BMW take a major prize, though they were often in the points. Geoff Duke, Dickie Dale and Fumio Ito all rode at World Championship level for BMW in the late 1960s, but their star rider was Walter Zeller. His and the factory's zenith was in 1956 when he finished second in the World Championship to John Surtees and his MV Agusta. However, the best race results he achieved were two second places. This was no mean achievement, but the whole thing

ABOVE: **The revolutionary 1000 cc BMW R100RS.**

must have seemed rather uninspiring to a global market of glory-seeking teenagers.

On three wheels, however, BMW were world beaters. In twenty-one years of competing in the World Sidecar Championship, BMW won an unbelievable nineteen times. The broad, flat-twin engine was ideal for low, fast cornering and its ability to haul the extra weight reliably was unmatched. But sidecars do not really cut the mustard with the majority of roadburners and, like it or not, it is the speed merchants who determine opinion.

BMW's external blank-faced stoicism bucked the trend of the rest of motorcycling culture. But beneath the steel-grey impassivity lurked cherry-pink embarrassment. The company felt ill-at-ease in the volatile market of motorcycle production. They tried to diversify into scooter production and failed. A three-wheeler project, the Isetta, was more successful but not enough to pull the company out of a downward spiral. By 1959, car and motorcycle sales were falling fast and the company went into the red. After a management reshuffle and a huge, sharp intake of breath from investors, BMW set off into the 1960s. But, as far as two wheels were concerned, nothing happened. It was BMW's new range of light sporty cars that saved the company from extinction.

The 1970s saw a resurgence of the BMW motorcycle marque. Largely, however, the drive was towards satisfying the needs of wealthy adherents of the large-capacity flat twin. There was also an unashamed desire to create a machine adapted to European taste and terrain. No radical redesign took place, but there were some significant improvements. Notably, the R90S was a restyled 900 cc (54 cu ins) superbike with a top speed of 200 km/h (125 mph).

Ironically, this essentially European bike started to rise in popularity in the United States. Japanese superbikes were becoming bizarrely big and heavy in the apparently endless search for more power. BMWs were now relatively light and had better handling.

The German desire to cater for the upmarket rider became even more clear in 1976. The 1000 cc (60 cu ins) R100RS came with a windtunnel-designed full-fairing and it was a mighty success. Despite being nearly twice the cost of its Japanese equivalents, it boasted many advantages. This was the first machine ever built where high-speed, day-long cruising was a serious and comfortable proposition.

BMW has gone on to produce a range of very successful off-road-style bikes based on their Paris-Dakar machines. They have also brought out their

RIGHT: **For a machine designed by an Englishman, this MZ Skorpion reeks of Germany.**

successful K series, which features a flat, in-line, three- or four-cylinder engine. With the crankshaft arranged along the length of the machine, there is no need to turn power-sapping right angles between it and the back wheel; the crankshaft, gearbox and drive shaft form one straight line. While the K series, and in particular the three-cylinder K75S, has many classic features, what it retains is essentially the touring image. What would blow away the BMW cobwebs is an all-out street racer. That they have yet to do.

And the "honour" of producing Germany's first street bike does not go to BMW, but to the most unlikely manufacturer. The emergence of an

BELOW: A rotary-valved
MZ 250 cc racer.

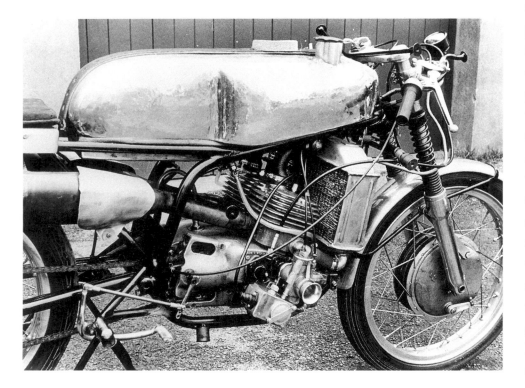

instant classic, a 600 cc (36 cu ins) single-cylinder, four-valve head, ultra-light café racer with raw, knee-trembling good looks, is courtesy of the producer of the world's least classic road machines – MZ. I say "road" machines because MZ were actually one of the top race teams of the late 1950s and early 1960s.

That MZ were the true pioneers of racing, two-stroke technology is all testimony to the innovative skill of their designer Walter Kaaden, because the company was *East* German and, thus, hopelessly underfunded. Throughout the mid to late 1950s, MZ, barred from international competition through lack of finance, begged, borrowed and traded their way into mainstream, world championship competition. Deprived of resources and facilities, Kaaden nevertheless made the first ever engine which developed the equivalent of 200 bhp per litre. His 1961, 25 bhp 125 cc (7 cu ins) single two-stroke was a brilliant lesson in simplicity. Its secret was the harnessing of disc-valve technology. A spinning disc with a cut-away section controlled the timing of the intake of mixture much more accurately and lengthened the inlet phase. Kaaden also shaped the exhaust of the MZ so that a resonating pressure pulse was timed to travel back down the exhaust to the chamber and help retain fresh charge before the port closed. MZ's home-grown rider, Ernst Degner, and Rhodesian Gary Hocking gave the 125 cc (7 cu ins) and 250 cc (15 cu ins) MZs a good showing in 1959, and the team had sporadic wins through 1960. However, 1961 looked like being MZ's year. Degner was lying in first place in the 125 cc (7 cu ins) World Championship with one round, in Sweden, to go. Then Degner defected, courtesy of the Japanese! With him went Kaaden's dream and the secrets of Kaaden's technology to Suzuki. In fact, the East German disc-valve and resonance technology was copied and only marginally improved upon by the Japanese for the following thirty years of Grand Prix racing. Kaaden, nevertheless, pushed forward with improving his machinery. In came watercooling and higher power and MZ peaked again in the 1964 250 cc (15 cu ins) World Championship with their English rider, Alan Shepherd, coming third overall. Shepherd had often been forced to compete the season alone, without Kaaden or his mechanics' support, because they were denied access to some Western countries.

With the collapse of the Berlin Wall, MZ are now reunited with the rest of Germany and the Western world. Renamed MuZ, they are on a ballistic trajectory. Their old range of machines are being phased out and a new MuZ Skorpion, with 600 cc (36 cu ins) sports Rotax engine and a 500 cc (30 cu ins) Roadster are in development. The machines represent a new wave in German industrial thinking.

The rapidly growing post-war internal market allowed Germany to thrive. With its dedication to quality, it made products which were then desirable outside its borders. But the Japanese have challenged the German industrial empire and found new ways to offer the same quality while offering a lighter, more dynamic touch at a lower price. It has taken Germany some time to respond to the threat. Now that a sacred cow like the Mercedes car is being seriously overhauled by the Japanese Lexus, the Germans are realizing that a new approach is needed. They have to sell in a world market and the old imperialism is no longer enough. The new MuZ motorcycles are part of this rennaissance, which is why the Skorpion – the hit of the Cologne Show – was actually created in Fulham, London by design company Seymour-Powell. The machine is designed to be built by the most basic of factories. The process of replacing the old Communist infrastructure will be a slow one. By utilizing aircraft glues to link elements of the frame together, welding is kept to a minimum. Everything does two jobs – the frame carries the oil and the seat is the airbox.

The new MuZ range still has to make it to the marketplace. Nevertheless, it is an exciting departure for German motorcycling, while still being a German machine through and through. The logic behind it is the Kaaden philosophy of simplicity, lightness and power; but more broadly, it represents the German principles of high-quality design and engineering, with heavy leanings towards aircraft technology. What it lacks is the reserve and reticence of earlier machines. This is no bad thing. If the Skorpion does make it into volume production, the boring label on German motorcycles may at last start to fade.

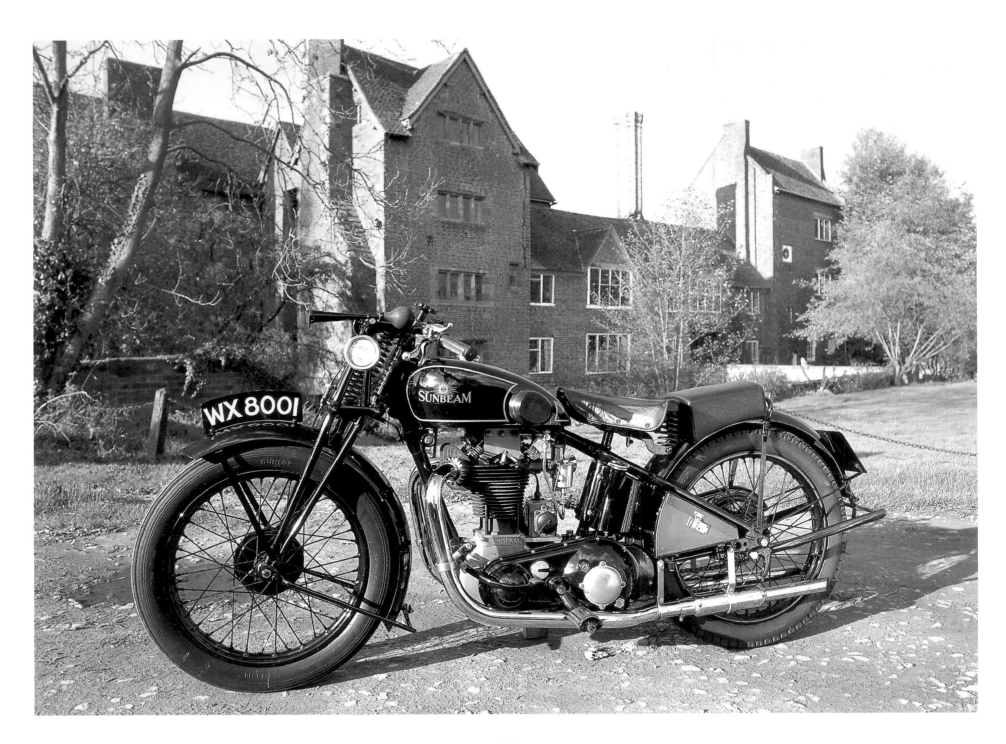

Britain used to be the workshop of the world. An imperial power which boasted the best engineering minds and inventions in the world – Stephenson and Kingdom-Brunel; steam engines, ships, bridges, and factories. "Made in Britain" had real meaning. Out of this gigantic manufacturing heritage grew a motorcycle industry which quickly outpaced its foreign competitors. From 1920 to 1960, the mighty British motorcycle industry ruled the roads. And then it all just blew away like sand in the wind.

Now, when many classic British motorcycles are remembered as oily, leaky and unreliable, it is as well to remember that the vast majority were nothing of the sort. Much of the problem for the British industry was that its machines were *too* good for the market. A lot of the bankruptcies in the 1920s, and again in the late 1950s and early 1960s, were because the company's products did not sell at a time when all the man-in-

ABOVE: **An AJS Big Port.**

OPPOSITE: **A Sunbeam Model 90.**

the-street could afford was cheap, simple transport.

For example, Sunbeam, the maker of beautiful black and gold machinery, won the 1920 Isle of Man TT with speeds of over 144 km/h (90 mph). They made the innovative Sunbeam 90 with an alloy piston, overhead valves set at 45 degrees and a centrally-positioned spark plug. Sunbeam spent the 1920s winning Grand Prix, but then faded with an outdated design. Their essentially gentleman's motorcycle had become too expensive and too old-fashioned. They were sold off in 1928 to ICI, and then in the 1930s to Associated Motorcycles who already owned AJS and Matchless.

AJS's great classic was the 350 cc (21 cu ins) Big Port. This was a radical design far ahead of its time – internal expanding brakes, all-chain drive and big-diameter exhaust, hence the name. It took the first three places in the 1921 Junior TT and

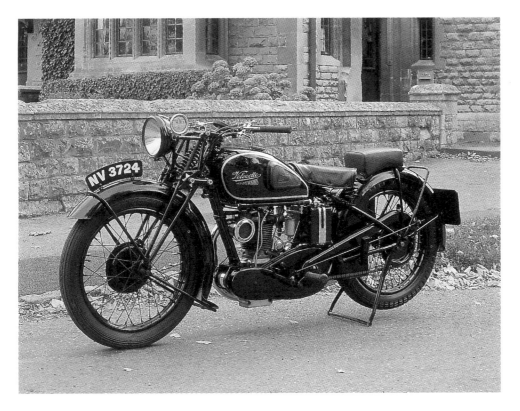

ABOVE: **A 1934 Velocette MK1 KTS Tourer.**

time. Worldwide motorcycle sales had plummeted throughout the 1960s; the market was just not big enough to support the business.

Velocette was a company typical of the many great names which had to endure ignominious humiliation. They had pioneered adventurous overhead cam models in the early 1920s and the race version won the Junior TT in 1926, 1928 and 1929. The roadgoing KSS, the legendary "Cammy" Velocette steadily became the 1920s and early 1930s boy-racer's favourite. The 500 cc (30 cu ins) Venom and the 350 cc (21 cu ins) Viper were single-cylinder sports models which did their fair share of café and club racing in the late 1950s. The Venom evolved into a major classic – the Velocette Venom Thruxton.

Velocette was a family-run business and had a close relationship with many private owners and tuners. Improvements by private individuals were fed back to the factory and willingly included in the following year's road models, so Velocette machinery was always of the highest quality. But Velocette were catering for only a small niche in the market at a time when survival meant volume. They tried to rectify this by bringing out the LE, but it was a commuter machine which lacked any sense of the styling the market was after. Velocette went out of business in 1971.

It is the greatest irony that in 1959, just as the decline was about to commence, more two-wheelers were registered than ever before in Britain. Exports from Britain to the USA were

then amazingly won the Senior TT for 500 cc (30 cu ins) machines. It broke the Senior average speed record at 87.2 km/h (54.5 mph).

AJS enjoyed a period of stability and success on race tracks around the world after the Second World War with their overhead-cam 7R. But, along with Norton and Matchless, they just petered out as Japan strode mercilessly onto the world stage.

By 1960, the British industry was in undiagnosed terminal decline. By 1970, it was on its deathbed. To those involved it must have felt like the walls suddenly fell down around them, but under the surface things had been tough for a long enormous, and for companies like Triumph, the USA was their largest market. Despite the fact that the majority of sales were mopeds, the customer base was there, and things should have been on an extremely solid rockbed. But by 1970, the Japanese had grabbed the lantern and its light burned brightly over Hammamatsu. It seemed that some Samurai warrior had crept in and executed the Anglo-Saxon Knights of the Road. Shocked cabinet ministers, such as Tony Benn, commissioned inquiries. Investors stood around in circles looking at their feet. People wrote books with titles like: *Whatever happened to the British Motorcycle Industry?* And from this end of the century, it looks like the British motorcycle Industry committed suicide.

What happened is extremely easy to see with hindsight. The underlying factors had disaster written all over them. A lot of tired, beleaguered people were up against it and, after a titanic struggle, had to give in. What is interesting is what kind of people they were and what they were up against. The collapse of the industry has more to do with questions of psychology and social forces than any shortcomings in design and technology. The answers to those questions lie in the motorcycles, in the best and the worst machines they made and the people who bought them.

The Vincent Black Shadow is a name laden with myth and lore. Produced for only nine years after the Second World War, by enthusiasts largely for affluent enthusiasts, it was justifiably advertized as "The World's Fastest Standard Motor Cycle".

Phil Vincent, the company's owner and a keen racer, had a powerful vision. In his eyes, quality of design and engineering came before quantity. His Australian designer, Phil Irving, conceived a machine which reached new limits of performance excellence. The Series A Vincent Rapide came out in 1937 as a 47-degree, 998 cc (60 cu ins) V-twin roadster. However, the big engine gave rise to a rather long wheelbase and the mass of external oilways earned the machine the nickname of the "plumber's nightmare".

The real classic Vincents actually took off nine years later, in 1946. The engine had become a stress-bearing element of the frame and the consequent loss of the front down tube took 7.7cm (3ins) off the wheelbase. The oilways had been rationalized and the cylinders given a 50-degree angle. The original concept had been for a long distance tourer, but the immense power and tractability of the 1000 cc (60 cu ins) Irving engine meant sports and racing models were inevitable. Made until 1955, the Series B, C and D Rapide tourers, the Black Shadow sports bikes and the Black Lightning racers were glorious beasts. They combined a raw, almost evil, power with a smooth sophistication that made them seem sinister, yet beguiling. The curious firing pattern, both cylinders firing close together followed by a gap like the galloping horse's gait, added to their animal persona. Top speeds of over 200 km/h (125 mph) on road models underlined their aggressiveness. In 1955, in line with his purist

LEFT: The basic
manufacturing systems
of the British industry,
in 1952.

The compulsive desire to cater for the enthu-siast has long been a feature of the British motor-cycling landscape and perhaps British manufacturing in general, but it is also a hazardous financial trap. There is a sense in which the British industrial mentality still cannot wholeheartedly embrace sell-ing for selling's sake. This deep-seated industrial psychology was laid down in the time of an expand-ing Empire when what was made was bought because it was *well* made. The throwback to the philosophy of "real men make things" has been a millstone round the British necks for the last forty years of international industrial competition. The fact that the great Triumph Meridan works have been replaced by a housing estate is a testimony to this phenomenon.

The great British motorcycle industry existed from around 1920 to 1970, but was essentially Victorian in character. In an earlier generation, Britain had been the unchallenged world centre of steam technology. In the climate of a *laissez-faire* political ethos, private, entrepreneurial engineering flourished. Individuals and small firms often grew out of the daring inventions of one man. As steam machinery proliferated, there arose a social and political need for the myriad manufacturers to come under central fiscal control. From this grew the great British penchant for standards and regulation. Standardization brought about the growth of the parts business, and many manufacturers began to use the same components. This permitted adaptability, reduced

ideals, when the market could not bear the high cost of the machines, Vincent simply stopped making them.

To be fair, in many ways the Vincents were ahead of their time. They were made at a time when motorcycles were down-market, and there was not an upper-class market as there is now for, say, BMW. The kind of people who now lay out many thousands of pounds for a Harley-Davidson did not exist in the 1950s, which is why a good Black Shadow can now fetch £15,000.

RIGHT: The first Series B
Vincent Black Shadow of
1948.

THE SIDECAR

The Brough Superior and the Vincent Rapide were, of course, for the pleasure of gentlemen. In the heydays of the British motorcycle, the average man was more likely to have a Triumph or a Royal Enfield attached to a sidecar. Sidecars were used for all sorts of trades. Companies like Shell and the RAC had fleets of patrolmen on combinations. The mass-produced small car did not take root for a long time in Britain. Unlike Ford in America, companies like Austin had to wait, because of four long years of war, to get machines like the Model Seven out in sufficient volume to the public. But the car threatened the combination only a little, as the Great Depression started to bite, and then the Second World War kept the car at bay. It was only when the Mini came out in the 1950s that the sidecar largely vanished and motorcycle sales started to plummet.

costs and made repair and servicing simple.

The two main psychological notions, then, that the steam era bequeathed to the petrol-powered generation were, firstly, that anyone with the requisite skills and resources could and should build their invention and, secondly, that using the best available parts was the nature of the game. These two ideas have had a huge effect on the evolution of British motorcycle design, and they reached their end-point in the Triton. There may be better British bikes, there may be more classic bikes, but the Triton is the quintessence of British motorcycling, in the strictest sense. You cannot buy a new Triton, there is no such thing. You make a Triton: it is half a Triumph and half a Norton. It is made out of bits – the "best" bits. The favourite combination is to take the running gear, suspension and wheels of a Norton with a Featherbed frame, and insert a Triumph Bonneville engine, a T110 or T120. The whole thing then gets generic clip-on handlebars, rearset footpegs, a racing seat and alloy petrol tank. (It is said that the whole trend started because Norton refused to sell anything other than whole motorcycles. When racing-car makers wanted a Manx Norton engine, they had to buy a whole machine and sell the cycle parts.) Whether all this makes the best bike is largely irrelevant. The fact that people did it and still do (and many more dream of doing it) is the point.

The Triton underlines absolutely the centrality to British motorcycling of hands-on engineering by the user. It embodies the British obsession with prototypes. Its hybrid nature is utterly dependent on a widespread network of craftsmen who make the specialist parts. To create a Triton takes skill. To own a Triton is to be yourself "one-off" and special. Its brute functionality eschews the mundane. It is a street racer. This is not transport, this is Death or Glory.

The Triton's heyday was the café racer era of the 1950s and 1960s. But long before the Rockers, the parts bins had also been scoured to

RIGHT: One of the many incarnations of the Triton spirit.

create what has been called the Rolls-Royce of motorcycles – the 1920s Brough Superior SS100. T E Lawrence (Lawrence of Arabia) had six. He named them Boanerges I to VI, after the twin Norse gods of fire. He died falling off one, trying to avoid hitting a butcher's delivery boy on a bicycle. The twin gods of fire referred to the Brough's 1000 cc (60 cu ins) JAP V-twin engine. Publicity-seeking George Brough brought together the best technology of the day to create the best possible machine, and by 1930, the leading model in the catalogue was the SS100 Alpine Grand Sports. It featured a 998 cc JAP V-twin engine by J A

by Edward Turner was an elegant solution to the problem of fitting a four-cylinder engine into a motorcycle. With chain-driven overhead camshafts and two centrally-geared crankshafts, and the drive taken off the rear, this was a superb motor. The initial 500 cc (30 cu ins) engine soon became a 600 cc (36 cu ins) unit. The 600 cc (36 cu ins) frame design was impressive and featured a central down-tube and duplex engine cradle. The whole thing had a very high standard of finish throughout. Later, the engine was taken out to 1000 cc (60 cu ins) and continued in production until 1958.

Similarly, Matchless had made many early classic machines, but the 1930 four-cylinder Silver Hawk, a direct competitor to the Ariel Square Four, was their attempt to create a machine for a market that hardly existed. Matchless were trying to find customers who wanted the smooth power of a car in the relatively lightweight, and hence sporty, motorcycle. The Silver Hawk's 600 cc (36 cu ins) engine was of great note; it arranged the four cylinders in a narrow V-shape and thus had only one crankshaft.

The Silver Hawk was an interesting product in a shrinking market. It never achieved the sales success of the Ariel Square Four and was discontinued in 1935. It seems to be a fact of motorcycling life that there can never be anything other than a tiny market for the two-wheeled equivalent of the Rolls-Royce.

Most factories satisfied themselves with a range of basic machines, topped off with a race-

Prestwich of Tottenham, London, Castle leading-link front forks, Bonniksen speedometer, Sturmey-Archer gearbox, Brooks saddle, Bentley and Draper rear springs, Lucas magdyno, Pilgrim oil pump, Amal carburettor … the list goes on. Brough's special formula was that of linking effective sub-contracting to the highest possible quality of build. He contributed nickel and then stainless steel, bulbous tanks, leather toolboxes and a mass of small, crafted parts. As a keen racer/rider he knew what the upmarket sports customer wanted. Giving the customer what they wanted in those days largely meant handbuilding bespoke machines in limited numbers for a premium price.

There were those, though, who tried to produce luxury motorcycles for a wider public. The 1930 500 cc (30 cu ins) Ariel Square Four designed

ABOVE: **An Ariel Square Four in uncharacteristic full-chat mode.**

OPPOSITE: **A gentleman's mount – the Brough Superior SS100.**

developed sportster. Many factories like Norton, BSA and Triumph produced masses of affordable small single- and twin-cylinder machines, but gained broader esteem by winning track or off-road competitions with their racing specials. The success message was then directly carried to the people by producing a limited range of expensive road models based closely on the racers. One or two big sportsters crawling around an average town would soon set people's minds racing.

One of the prime exponents of this philopso-phy was Norton. Norton is probably the greatest name in motorcycling in the world; a bold claim, but its history is remarkable. It is a name, although struggling, which still exists, and continues to innovate and win races. It has dominated every sphere of competition and was a large-scale producer of popular and classic machinery for nearly ninety years. Even the mighty Honda is still only touching fifty.

Norton's race-winning exploits sold the production machinery right from the start. The company was created by James Lansdown Norton in 1898 and moved into motorcycle production in 1902, first making Clement-Garrard powered machines and then the Norton Energette. The early years were very much about building machines to customers' specifications. The first real production Nortons were a range of Peugeot-engined models in 1906, including, importantly, a V-twin.

It was the 660 cc (40 cu ins) V-twin Norton which won the multi-cylinder class of the first Isle of Man Tourist Trophy race in 1907. This accolade sold Nortons for many years, despite the fact that the firm had to wait nearly twenty years to repeat the achievement. Nortons sold their side-valve machines, in particular the 16H, from 1912 onwards on the basis of successes at Brooklands. It was 1922 before they introduced their popular and successful overhead-valve 500 cc (30 cu ins) single, the Model 18. The OHV machine was given the full race build-up with attempts on the British and International Flying Kilometre speed records. At Brooklands, against a strong wind, Rex Judd took the Norton to 143.87 km/h (89.92 mph). Unfortunately, the record only lasted for a few hours because Norton were ousted by an OHV Douglas on the same day. Nevertheless, in 1924, a near-standard Model 18 brought Norton the glory they had been waiting for. On a machine with rear brakes designed for the Ford Model T car, Alec Bennett took his Norton to victory in the Senior Isle of Man TT, breaking the average speed barrier of 96 km/h (60 mph). Norton also won that year's sidecar event. Soon orders for the 18 were out-stripping supply.

At this time, James Lansdowne Norton, never in the greatest of health, was becoming ill and had only a year to live. Nevertheless, he was still furi-ously working away to improve his machinery. Notably, he patented an overhead-cam design dri-ven by chain, which both opened and closed the valves mechanically – an early example of the desmodronic principle! After his death in April

1925, the company was joined by the great Stanley Woods who promptly won the 1926 Senior TT for them, again with a pushrod, overhead valve model. It is interesting to note that as a Norton employee, Woods was a racer in the summer and worked as a salesman in the winter.

The following year, an overhead cam version of the 18 won the Isle of Man TT with Alec Bennett riding. The road-going replica, the CS1, went on sale later the same year. While the engine was not a high revver, it had phenomenally smooth, low-end great power and could do 160 km/h (100 mph)!

LEFT: Alec Bennett after winning the 1927 TT, on his 490 cc Norton CS1.

From then on, the CS1 was steadily overhauled by four-valve-head Rudges, and so Norton designers Joe Craig and Arthur Carroll set about improving their machinery. They retained a two-valve head, although the valves were considerably larger, and eventually the machine got a shortened frame, down-draught carburettor and a Sturmey-Archer, four-speed, positive-stop gearbox. They had created a machine soon to be known as the "International", and with it three decades of race track glory. In 1931, Norton swept the board with the first three places in the Senior TT and first, second and fourth in the Junior. They also won most of the European road races. The road-going replicas – the 350 cc (21 cu ins) Model 40 and 500 cc (30 cu ins) Model 30 were launched in 1932 to great acclaim.

The same basic design kept Norton on top for a long time. However, after the Second World War, teams like Velocette and AJS often got the better of Norton, and so new measures were required. The design which led Norton to reassert its racetrack dominance was to become an icon of British motorcycle design – the Featherbed frame. Designed by Rex McCandless in Belfast, the double-loop frames with rear-swinging-arm suspension were first tried out in 1950 and were an instant sensation. Norton newcomer Geoff Duke won the Senior TT, and Artie Bell the Junior; Nortons took the first three places in both races. Geoff Duke was beaten into second place in the 500 cc (30 cu ins) World Championship that year by Umberto Masetti on a Gilera. Most of the British team's problems had

centred on tyres and a late-season switch to Avon changed their luck. In 1951, Duke won both the 350 cc (30 cu ins) GP and 500 cc (30 cu ins) GP world championships and had a double in the Senior and Junior TT.

This great era spawned what the enthusiasts had long hoped for – a Norton roadster with a Featherbed frame. The Dominator de Luxe with a 500 cc (30 cu ins) twin-cylinder engine was launched in 1951, but was not available to the British public until 1955.

By the mid-1950s, Norton's policy of using race machines to evolve the next season's production machinery was starting to hit problems. The trend in racing was for an ever-increasing use of streamlining, a style which, at the time, was not desirable to the road user. At the same time, money for racing was shrinking along with decreasing sales. Cheap cars were the problem. The team was also losing to multi-cylinder European machines, so Norton pulled out of road-racing. The company's sales vanguard was thereafter based on its over-the-counter racers, especially the Manx. The year 1955 saw the discontinuation of the ancient side-valve models and the Model 18 and the introduction of the Model 88 Dominator, the first Featherbed twin for home consumption. In 1956 it was joined by the 99, a 600 cc (36 cu ins) version.

The Suez Crisis and the subsequent petrol rationing suggested that utility motorcycles would be ever more popular. In 1958, Norton, therefore, introduced the Jubilee, a 250 cc (15 cu ins) twin tourer with semi-enclosure. It did not sell well, and it appalled the purists who thought Norton should only be turning out roadburners. This dilemma startled the British motorcycle industry like a rabbit in a car's headlights. The existing customers wanted the hands-on, race-honed machinery they were used to; the wider market,

economic reality and the arrival of the Japanese suggested the opposite. The British never really got to grips with the latter.

In 1960, the Jubilee was joined by the 350 cc (21 cu ins) Navigator. In 1961, the big machines were re-presented as SS, Sports Specials. They were essentially 500 cc (30 cu ins) and 600 cc (37

BELOW: One of the last British classics, the Norton Commando.

cu ins) Dominators with hotter cams and twin carburettors. They were soon joined by a 650 cc (40 cu ins), and eventually a 750 cc (45 cu ins) version, the Atlas. This machine sold well but nevertheless the decline continued. Most of Norton's production was going to the United States. Norton's owners since 1953, Associated Motor Cycles, AMC, had debts of over £2 million and were taken over in 1966 by the Villiers Group. The Norton range was savagely cut to the 650SS and the 750 cc (45 cu ins) Atlas.

Then in 1967, Norton pulled one last trick out of the bag – the Commando. In over ten years of production the Commando was voted "Machine of the Year" five times by the readers of *Motor Cycle News*. It was essentially a 750 cc (45 cu ins) Atlas engine rubber-mounted in a duplex frame. Cleverly, the rear swinging arm was mounted onto the rear of the gearbox to form an isolated drive train. Vibration was thus massively reduced. The Commando was updated throughout its life and sold very well in the United States. Despite the model's success, Norton Villiers Triumph went into liquidation in 1975 and ceased production in 1978.

The third name in the ill-fated triumvirate is one which also spans the century and is once again in production – Triumph. In 1992, Triumph sold 300 new machines to Japan.

The company was started by a German, Siegfried Bettmann, and sold Triumph bicycles from 1886. His partner, another German, Mauritz

Schulte fitted a Belgian Minerva $2\frac{1}{4}$ hp engine to a bicycle and the first Triumph motorcycle was born. By 1905, the company was making its own 3 hp engine and the business took off. The most notable Triumph of the pioneer period was the Model H which had a three-speed, Sturmey Archer countershaft gearbox and belt drive to the back wheel; 30,000 were supplied to the War Office in the First World War.

Triumph entered the 1920s in an immensely powerful position, financially speaking. They had a reputation for producing solid, reliable machines. The "Trusty Triumph", it has been argued, saved the motorcycle from oblivion, at a time in the pioneer period when the public were becoming tired of other manufacturers' machines which were utterly troublesome. The 1920s was a period of stoical volume production for the company. The Priory Street works in Coventry was dedicated to churning out unremarkable machines for the average man at a time when the demand for personal transport was high. The first notable variation on this theme came when Sir Harry Ricardo's four-valve head was introduced in 1921, but it was little more than a pre-war machine with the four-valve head grafted on.

The mark of Triumph's 1920s success was the output of nearly 1,000 machines a week. Demand was highest for the Model P, a fairly good machine at the very cheap price of £42 17s 6d. However, the decade which had started with optimism, ended in financial disaster. With the Great

Depression in full flow, the company's fortunes plummeted. Sales were down, the range of models on offer had had no development for seven or eight years. The car side of the business was taking precedence, because of the possible wider profit margins. Designer Val Page arrived from Ariel and immediately got the design side running again. He created a series of designs which were totally unlike predecessors of the same name. But his efforts had little effect on the company's fortunes and it went into receivership in 1936. Page left to join BSA. Jack Sangster, the owner of Ariel, bought the motorcycle interest and so the Triumph car and motorcycle separated in all but name. Sangster put his head designer at Ariel in charge – Edward Turner.

Turner's key achievements for the business were to create stylish, streamlined machines while cost-cutting and manufacturing more efficiently to achieve greater profits. He was given no money for reinvestment, so everything had to be rationalized. Existing machinery had to be used, existing models had to be built upon. Taking the basic Val Page-designed 500 cc (30 cu ins), 350 cc (21 cu ins) and 250 cc (15 cu ins) singles, he turned them into the world-beating Tigers. Their sleek proportions made them an instant hit. Turner's restyling of the Triumph range showed that he was listening to the market.

He was also a gifted designer and went on to create the famous Speed Twin. In this he was influenced by the Square Four which he had worked on

ABOVE: A 1939 model, Triumph Speed Twin. Usually only available in Amaranth Red, this black version was produced to special order.

at Ariel and by Val Page's 1933 Triumph 650 twin. The new vertical 500 cc (30 cu ins) Twin's performance, smoothness, ease-of-starting and control made it very popular. Much of its popularity lay in the fact that it was a good all-rounder – it was very tuneable and could be raced in club events on tarmac or grass at the weekends, and then provide reliable transport through the week. This was an attractive feature as most riders could only afford one machine at the time. Turner's policy, born out of necessity, was to keep factory retooling costs to a minimum. The Triumph Twin and small single were its staple output for thirty years. Their evolution, however, was impressive.

Just before the Second World War, Triumph brought out the Tiger 100, a sports version which came with a Certificate of Performance. The 100

ABOVE: **A T160 Triumph Trident.**

after the Second World War meant American taste dictated design policy to a large extent. The Americans wanted cc's. The result, in line with Turner's conservative philosophy, was a 650 cc (40 cu ins) version of the Speed Twin – the 6T, the Thunderbird. An added bonus was the introduction of a rear-sprung hub, which offered springing without radical redesign and hence cost.

The most famous Triumph of all, though, is the Bonneville, the T120. Introduced in 1959 as a twin-carb version of the 650 twin, it soon got a duplex cradle frame and new front forks. It was a street racer which carried off many production competition honours throughout the 1960s.

The greatest irony of the Triumph story is that just as the going was starting to get impossible, a machine appeared on the horizon that might have saved them. The 750 cc (45 cu ins), three-cylinder Trident was almost an accident. A 1963 prototype, basically a Tiger and a half, was created as a stop-gap, while a completely new machine was designed. The prototype was so powerful that the project could not be dropped, but management hesitation and production teething problems resulted in the bike only appearing in 1968. While it won at Daytona in 1971 and sold well in the States for a short time, it was blown away by the Honda CB750. It was the beginning of the end.

The other major British casualty, of course, was BSA. In their heyday, the Small Heath factory in Birmingham used to employ over 12,000 people. The company had been formed as the Birmingham

tag was supposed to indicate speeds achieved at the Brooklands track although whether they ever did is not clear. Many other manufacturers got in on the vertical twin act after the war, but Triumph were first out of the blocks. Triumph won the Manx Grand Prix in 1946 with Ernie Lyons on board. The secret of the success was an unlikely one. The Tiger's cast-iron cylinder and head were replaced by alloy ones from Triumph-made Lancaster Bomber generator engines.

The 500 cc (30 cu ins) was generally regarded as the optimum size for the vertical twin, giving enough power and acceleration without incurring too much of a vibration penalty. However, the tremendously successful export drive to America

Small Arms Company in 1861. BSA soon added cycle manufacture to their list of products and by 1905 were making frames which could be fitted with small engines. From its first full motorcycle in 1909, BSA proceeded through the pioneer years in fine fashion with a series of sturdy machines and average performances in the Isle of Man TT. The war was a busy one for BSA, and they emerged exhausted into the 1920s. A massive effort to win

BELOW: **The boy-racer's dream – the BSA Gold Star DBD34.**

the TT in 1921 with a new overhead-valve model ended in embarrassment with all eight entries failing to finish. This put the management off road-racing for a while and they concentrated on gaining publicity through off-road and long-distance trials.

The important BSA of the late 1920s was the Sloper. Up until then, BSA had been solid if unexciting. The 500 cc (30 cu ins) S27 overhead-valve Sloper changed all that. The Sloper was solid but

energetic. The first action-packed BSAs, though, really started to emerge in the 1930s with the arrival of the upright, single-cylinder "Star" series. Assisted by a win in the International Six Days Trials, the 28 bhp, 500 cc (30 cu ins) Blue Star and subsequent Empire Stars started a BSA trend for thumping singles. Val Page's side-valve M series of 1937 onwards were a familar facet of British motorcycling for over twenty-five years. The M series engines were bullet-proof, a perfect partner for the big duplex cradle frame. The flexibility of the design meant that it was equally at home in road or off-road exploits. And the cream of the crop was the legendary Gold Star. The 1938 M24 Gold Star was an alloy-engined version of the M23 Empire Star. In race trim it could top 160 km/h (100 mph) and was named after the Brooklands gold star awarded to racers who averaged over that speed on the banked, oval track during a race. The 1937 version pumped out 28 bhp and improved gradually up until the DBD34 Gold Star Clubman of 1956 was capable of 42 bhp. This machine, manufactured until 1963, was developed by continuous racing in trials, scrambles and, from 1947, in Clubman's road events. The Clubman event at the Isle of Man TT was started in 1947 to encourage more people to participate in the sport. The race was only open to true production models, and to qualify, 200 models had to have been built. From 1949, the Junior event was won by the Gold Star every year until its termination in 1956.

BSA, which had long sold its large range of

smaller machines on the basis of its solidly reliable trials-conquering exploits, suddenly had a winner on their hands. The fact that it was successful in all forms of the sport made it attractive to the public who felt they could buy a potential production racer off the shelf, in much the same way as people buy Japanese sports bikes today. Unlike other companies' loss-leader machinery, the Gold Star actually made a profit. It was outstanding aesthetically and the engine's power curve and tractability made it a joy to ride. The big single-cylinder made your guts rumble joyously although it could be hell to start. For a great many people it is the all-time popular British classic.

Machines like the BSA Gold Star, the Norton Dominator and the Triumph Bonneville were what Britain was good at. They allowed the British motorcycle industry to develop a sense of its own supremacy that was to be its ultimate downfall. The wide range of commuter machinery which these "superbikes" led, had many of their technical features. That meant the small bikes were still essentially for the use of knowledgeable riders. Features which were likely to impress the non-motorcyclist were frowned upon; that was left to the Japanese.

Behind all the British industry's early innovative flair there was a Midlands obstinacy and boorishness which grew more prevalent with time. Triumph's Edward Turner, for example, had a "tighten-your-belt" philosophy which he followed religiously and it served him and his employers well for many years. Hunger had made Turner create a great lineage of machines, totally in tune with market demands. The riches he got as a result turned him into an isolated figure. His violent temper and dislike of being proved wrong created a very difficult climate for internal change.

He was not alone. The attitude of the management of Triumph, Norton and BSA was utterly dismissive of the customer. It often took months for a machine to be delivered. Reg Gilbert, now a South-London Honda dealer, once ordered an AJS and got so fed up with waiting that he went round to the Woolwich factory to see what was happening. On arrival, he found rows of finished machines awaiting their petrol tanks: the man who did the gold lining on the tanks was off sick and so no machines were leaving the factory.

This sort of escapade was not entirely the fault of management. Many of the owners had taken large dividends out of the companies at a time when Japanese manufacturers were borrowing heavily and investing in the best possible modern technology. Up until the collapse of the early 1970s, the British motorcycle was largely built on the lathe – general-purpose machinery which had been in use for decades. The result was poor reliability at a time when the Japanese were making very high-quality machines.

While the wider economic conditions of the 1960s and 1970s were no doubt appalling, some reinvestment and understanding of the market might have meant that the British motorcycle industry could have survived like the Italians and Americans, selling on outstanding heritage aspects. The present tentative efforts of the new Triumph marque could have attracted even greater backing if the line had been unbroken, but for that to have happened a lot of very proud people would have had to admit they were wrong. And the gentry who governed the great industry in 1950s were not going to admit to that.

It is almost as if the British fought the war to preserve their Victorian engineering heritage and methodologies. Great ideas in the UK have often been hamstrung by the past; a crippling nostalgia haunts manufacturing thinking. The problem, in a nutshell, is investor confidence. In British motorcycle design there were great advances in the early 1920s because there was some money around and both the investors and the designers could have some of the cake. The same was true just after the Second World War when people needed cheap transport. The decline of the 1960s started when the masses began to be able to afford the small car. British owners and investors did not have the guts to take the motorcycle industry onto a new stage of development, but the Japanese did.

Japan, free from old ideologies and supported by a growing internal market, did not bother to look back. They looked forward and asked: "How can we create a new world motorcycle market?" It took a lot of investment and courage, but it worked.

FIRE FROM THE EAST

The Japanese now hold court in the palace of world motor-cycling, where once sat the British. Their empire is built on four pillars – Honda, Suzuki, Yamaha and Kawasaki. The name Honda is almost a synonym for "motorcycle". It is the largest and most powerful of the four. Large is an understatement: in its forty-five years of production, Honda has produced 60 million motorcycles, not to mention cars and static engines. Honda's history is the spine of Japanese motorcycling, but many people do not realize that the company is Japanese. There is a story, perhaps apocryphal, of an American mother who wanted to get her son a Honda because she did not want him riding around on a Japanese bike: the implication being that Japanese motorcycles are cheap and badly-made, whereas Honda means quality. What Honda and the other manufacturers represent now is the highest-quality engineering and design on a massive scale.

Many classic enthusiasts, however, begrudge the Japanese any accolade. To those people, the

ABOVE: A Yamaha
RD350LC.

OPPOSITE: The Honda
CBR900R Fireblade – the
name says it all.

Japanese will always be cheap copyists with an eye for a quick yen, although the plain truth is that Japan reinvigorated a dying industry in the 1960s, advanced design and engineering standards and made motor-cycling respectable again. In the process, they created a whole array of classic machines.

The top-of-the-range machines that are now seen flying around the streets like plastic cigarette packets may seem like the last thing that one could call "classic". Yet machines like the Honda Fireblade are so much about affluent Western culture that it is hard to believe that they will not be seen in retrospect as a supremely complex mix of technology and aesthetics for an indulgent age. In fact, they may be the final examples of the species – Japan is possibly coming to the end of its classic era. The top Japanese machines of today may be destined to become one of the last great icons of the late twentieth century. They outstrip virtually every car and bike on the road, accelerating from 0 to 96 km/h (0 to 60 mph) in less than 2.5 seconds

125

and with top speeds of over 250 km/h (160 mph). They are essentially mid-1980s engineering and design excellence gone mad. Faceless bureaucrats want these bikes off the roads because they are simply too fast and too much fun. They may have no place in the new millennium; the world recession is steering motorcycle design on a new path — but more of that later.

The personas of the modern Japanese superbikes were designed to appeal to 1980s monetarist values — symbols of individualist power and freedom. The Honda Fireblade, the Suzuki GSXR-1100, the Kawasaki ZXR 750, the Yamaha FZR-1000 EXUP had to be more than examples of great engineering design. They had to work as well as any machine, to be at the cutting edge in technology terms, but they also had to work hard aesthetically. They were created to excite; as soon as you look at them, a whole stream of messages have to be conveyed simultaneously and coherently — the fact that they are fast, that they are light, that they are state-of-the-art, that they are superdynamic. While this may not seem like the stuff of classic engineering, for a product today to be a powerful seller, even in a post-monetarist era, the aesthetic component is essential.

The first obvious aesthetic component is that Japanese sports bikes bear a very close resemblance to Formula One race bikes, much more so than sports cars do to Formula One racing cars. Throughout its history, the sports motorcycle has always been a mythological beast, a magic race-

horse that vanquishes all in its path. Its ancestor was the young cad's stallion, and it still retains the knees-tucked-up riding position and the low tight reins. The Japanese have recognized this fundamental quality and have exploited it. Japanese designers wage a constant, high-profile war to satisfy a basic demand for near-race-level performance on the road. To understand why they do this, it is necessary to go back and discover the man who made it all possible.

The Japanese had their home-grown pioneer era about forty-five years later than everyone else. Before the Second World War, there had been a watered-down version of what was happening in the rest of the motorcycling world: a few one-off prototypes around the beginning of the century, importation of British and German machines, the building of Harley-Davidsons under licence, shortlived attempts at domestic production and a few regular races was the sum total of the Japanese scene. The war, however, set everything back to zero.

Japan was literally flattened after the war. It suffered much worse devastation than any other country with its cities reduced to rubble, and its largely agrarian/military society in tatters. The population was starving; city dwellers had to travel out to the surrounding fields to scavenge for food, and many travelled by bicycle. An impoverished engineer, however, saw an opportunity in this and he bought 200 war-surplus generator engines and attached them to bicycles. The machines soon sold out, many to black marketeers who wanted to get around quickly with their wares.

The entrepreneur's little home village of Komyo in Hammamatsu was swallowed up by the industrial sprawl he initiated. He was a prime force in the meteoric economic rebirth of his country. An empire bears his name – Soichiro Honda. Honda was a latter-day Henry Ford; he had a fire in his belly for engineering excellence and an obsession with producing the best possible motor-cycles for the masses. As a lateral thinker he was a maverick who woke up a deeply conformist society.

In the West, the stereotype image of a Japanese engineer is that of a very rule-bound, de-individu-alized drone. This is far from true; Honda was a real tearaway. He liked to party, drink, always wore loud, garish beach shirts and used to hit engineers with spanners if they did something wrong. Like all great chief executives, he spent a lot of time on the shop floor. He knew his employees and never dis-tanced himself from them. Above all, he listened to people and gave their ideas and designs a chance.

Honda was born in 1906, the son of a black-smith, and was apprenticed as a car mechanic at the age of sixteen. He opened his own garage and then, with little specialized knowledge or resources, started his own piston-ring manufacturing company in 1937. After the war, he sold out to Toyota and took a year off. He spent most of the time drinking and gambling, but all the time he was listening to people's dreams and thinking about how he could satisfy their desires.

Honda became the largest motorcycle produc-er in the world because of a vision – that of linking highest-quality engineering and mass-production with ease-of-use for the customer. In this way, he was mirroring the thinking of Vespa and Lambretta in Italy. After the initial venture with the generator engines on bicycles, he made his first complete machine, appropriately titled the "Dream". The 1949 Model D is now a priceless rarity. At a time when other Japanese manufacturers were still offering bicycles with clip-on engines, Honda had produced the first complete, "from scratch", Japanese post-war motorcycle. The Dream had a pressed-steel frame, a 98 cc (6 cu ins) two-stroke engine and a two-speed gearbox. This was closely followed by a 146 cc (8 cu ins) four-stroke, the Model E. Together, the Models sold well and the company began to grow. This was due, in no small part, to Honda's new business partner, Takeo Fujisawa. While Honda takes much of the credit for designing the products and creating the company philosophy, Fujisawa is the brains of the business who knocked the dealership and sales network into shape in those all-important early years.

However, Honda still wanted to satisfy the masses and he decided on a bicycle-based design for his Model F, the Cub. Much more sophisticated than its predecessor, it was exactly what the market and the company wanted: a reliable, cheap runabout which sold in large numbers. The machine was the first step to volume production – a key strand in the Honda success story – and it provided the financial rockbed for much greater technical advances.

As the company progressed through the 1950s, it met with severe financial problems and a lot of union trouble. Heavy investment required a massive turnover and was seriously affecting profitability. Honda and Fujisawa got down on their knees and asked the bank and the workforce

for patience and help. With suppliers' support, the company literally manufactured their way out of trouble, building and selling a new improved Dream.

By 1958, Honda's growing range of machines had swamped the domestic market and the company, in urgent need of a bigger return on its outlay,

BELOW: Soichiro Honda's first proper motorcycle – the Model D, the "Dream".

turned to exportation. With a Japanese reputation abroad for second-rate products, Honda knew that only international race success would attract global customers. His target was the toughest race in the world – the Isle of Man TT. Another strand of the Honda success story was about to be woven.

Honda came in 1959 and were sixth, seventh, eighth and eleventh in the 125 cc (7 cu ins) event. In 1960 they were fourth, fifth and sixth in the 250 cc (15 cu ins) event. At only the third attempt, Honda achieved their goal. The secret of their success was the multi-cylinder, high-revving, four-stroke technology as pioneered by the German team, NSU, in the early 1950s. Honda's 1961 125 cc (7 cu ins), parallel twin developed 20 bhp at 13,000 rpm and the four-cylinder, 250 cc (15 cu ins) developed 40 bhp at 14,000 rpm. With the young Mike Hailwood on board, the Honda 250 cc (15 cu ins) won the Lightweight TT and the 125 cc (7 cu ins) Honda won the Ultra Lightweight. Hailwood won the 250 cc (15 cu ins) World Championship and fellow Honda rider, Tom Phillis, the 125 cc (7 cu ins) World Championship that year too.

With those victories, Honda had earned themselves an entrance ticket to European showrooms. In 1961, the British industry offered the lightweight commuter market oily, badly-made, functional designs that were unreliable and troublesome. Motorcycle sales were in a slump. Honda's well-made small bikes revitalised the market. The Honda C92, of 1959 design, started to appear

RIGHT: A great Honda trio
– Jim Redman, Mike
Hailwood and Tom Phillis
after the 1961 250 cc Isle of
Man TT.

abroad in significant numbers in 1960. It featured a 125cc (7 cu ins) four-stroke engine, pressed-steel frame and pressed-steel, leading-link forks. Notably, it was sold as an advanced ride-to-work bike in a complete package which included the indicators, decent brakes, mirror and enclosed rear chain. Its main features were that it was very reliable and economical to ride.

It was quite different to anything on the market at the time. It had square headlamps, bright colours and often white-walled tyres. Right

from the start, Honda was trying to make a clean, socially-acceptable type of motorcycle with a broad appeal, but this was not just a styling trick. At a time when many British bikes had to have the throttle flipped incessantly to keep them from stalling, the Honda ticked over happily on its own. The engines were tightly engineered, there were no oil leaks and the quality of manufacture was excellent. Many testers and cynics tried hard to run the machines into the ground but they just kept going. While they were not exactly mind-shattering, they were certainly good value for money. But Honda knew he had to get the backing of the cognescenti, the street speed-freaks. Soon, the world saw the Honda CB92, a 125 SuperSport. It immediately hit the headlines as being by far the fastest 125 cc (7 cu ins) road bike that had been around for a long time. It brought with it many features from the race track – a twin leading-shoe front brake and a very

fast-revving, twin-cylinder, overhead-camshaft engine. It also carried the title "Benly", a name later to be associated with rather sedate Hondas. This is interesting because the word in Japanese means "convenience". Even in his early sports machines, Honda was thinking of ease-of-use for the customer.

Dave Dixon, the first British journalist to ride one, remembers:

RIGHT: **Mike Hailwood at the 1967 West German Grand Prix.**

The first one I saw and the first one I rode was one which the Japanese mechanics had taken to the Isle of Man in 1959. They used this as a runabout and my eyes lit on it and I asked if could I borrow it for a few hours and it was unbelievable. It had a maximum speed of about 112 km/h (70 mph), with me sitting upright on it. The brakes on it were incredible. They were better than most racing machines we'd had. The technology was outstanding, the method of manufacture, their die-castings, the quality of finish. These people were very serious about engineering. They took engineering concepts a megastep forward.

Such an accolade from a respected writer had a substantial effect on the attitudes of British riders,

ABOVE: **A two-wheeled revolution – the 1962 250 cc Honda CB72.**

although there was a hardcore who wanted to dismiss it. That became more difficult when the CB92's big brother hit the shores. The 250 cc (15 cu ins) CB72, with twin carburettors, could pump out 24 bhp at 9,000 rpm. In comparison, the 1964 Royal Enfield Continental GT 250 cc (15 cu ins) single was giving 21 bhp. While the Honda had its faults, it was certainly on an equal footing. It had all sorts of little treats for the boy-racer: adjustable foot pegs could be moved back for that all important racetrack feel. Price and reliability, however, meant such machines made huge inroads into European and American sales.

In just over a decade, Honda had become the largest motorcycle manufacturer in the world with annual sales of over one million machines. This rise to pre-eminence mirrored and often led Japanese post-war growth. In a country with no natural resources, survival had been dependent on communal effort. A key ingredient in their rebirth was that people worked hard. Unhindered by a Victorian manufacturing legacy and backed by American War Aid and import controls, they had the chance get it right from the start.

Honda's use of scale was built upon in the 1960s in a way that had never been seen before. They used expansion to build new factories that had innovative techniques for the time: transfer lines, automated conveyors for assembly, special-purpose machinery rather than general-purpose machinery, new techniques of casting and forging. Many of the manufacturing machines were made by Honda themselves. With supreme self-confidence, they carried out very aggressive investment during the high growth years of the 1960s and took on very large levels of debt. But with that investment they achieved very low cost positions, very high margins, and were able to pay back the debt very quickly. In the end, they had higher profitability than the rest of the world's motorcycle industry. By comparison, the British industry of the time was much more interested in short-term profitability, whereas the Japanese were investing for longer-term returns and were taking less dividends.

The Japanese were also determined to give the customer more — features like push button electrics soon started to appear on their machines. In the process, they were modernizing motorcycling. The Doubting Thomases, nevertheless, scoffed that the Japanese could only make little machines; the

LEFT: **The big "Black Bomber" – the Honda CB450.**

Europeans and the Americans made the real stuff, the big machines.

Then, in 1965, Honda brought out its CB450. Their largest machine to date, its 43 bhp was only 4 bhp short of a 650 cc (40 cu ins) Triumph Bonneville. The twin-carb, double-overhead cam,

BELOW: Ring-a-ding-ding – a swinging-sixties Suzuki T20, known as the "Super Six".

parallel twin was in fact quite softly tuned and a comfortable and predictable ride. The machine was dubbed the "Black Bomber" by the British importers. While it never achieved massive sales, it did serve notice of Honda's intentions.

Faced with such a threat, foreign competitors resorted not to innovation but to ridicule. The slander was redoubled and the old favourite of "copying" was hurled around. But this had little effect on the Japanese. As Richard Seymour has pointed out, the word for "learn" and the word for "copy" in Japanese are the same. For example, in judo or kendo, one studies a series of pre-set moves, to be repeated again and again until mastered. Only when these pre-established prototypes are perfected can you move on to extemporize, to develop. There are three phases in Japanese thinking – copy, improve, dominate. The early Japanese motorbikes were copies, but the Japanese have been in the "dominate" phase for a long time now.

Spurred on by Honda's example, the other Japanese manufacturers were not slow to catch up. Suzuki were also from the Hammamatsu area. Not for the first time, fishing played its part in motor-cycling history (see the Harley-Davidson story, p. 48). Michio Suzuki was born in 1887 and his main business was silk loom production for many years. In 1950, a strike at the works sent him off on his bicycle with a fishing rod. The long, hard slog convinced him that the rising motorized bicycle market was worth exploring. He made a clip-on for sale in 1951 and went on to specialize

ABOVE: **The first superbike – the Honda CB750.**

LEFT: **Four pipes – big fun.**

in two-stroke manufacture for nearly twenty years. His Colleda models were heavily influenced by German machines, notably Adlers. Suzuki technology was given a hike up to world-class level when they helped East German Ernst Degner of MZ to defect in 1961.

Suzuki, nevertheless, achieved wide acclaim with its T20 Super Six, first introduced into Britain in 1966. It marked out a new era of two-stroke production and was claimed to be the first 250 cc (15 cu ins) motorcycle to reach 160 km/h (100 mph). It had a six-speed gearbox, which enabled the engine to make the most of its 29 bhp. It also featured pump lubrication, a horizontally-split crankcase, and a twin leading-shoe front brake. At the time, it knocked the spots off the competition, and it was soon being raced in almost standard trim. It would give bikes like the 650 cc (40 cu ins) Triumph Bonneville a very good run for its money.

Yamaha were also pushing forward down the two-stroke route, while Honda kept its allegiance to four-strokes. Yamaha, a brand owned by Nippon Gakki, a major musical instrument manufacturer, were enticed into motorcycle manufacture after the Second World War. Their president, Kaichi Kawakami, like Honda, was a firm believer in teamwork and product excellence. To create the Yamaha YA1 in 1955, the company's team of engineers took apart and recreated in its own image the German DKW RT125, the machine which was used as a pattern for lightweight two-strokes from a dozen manufacturers round the world, including the BSA Bantam.

Yamaha put an enormous effort into Grand Prix racing which took them quickly through their improvement phase. By 1965, they were offering the global market the YDS3, a strong competitor in the 250 cc (15 cu ins) stakes. Like the Suzuki, it

had a twin leading-shoe front brake, had a five-speed gearbox and, despite being under par on power, sold very well. By the mid-1960s, the other Japanese manufacturers were catching up on Honda's lead. For the big three – Honda, Yamaha, and Suzuki, (Kawasaki, part of a huge, heavy industrial company, was a late starter) – the game was

RIGHT: **The rubber-framed Kawasaki Mach III.**

racetracks. Yet, it delivered a very smooth 67 bhp and its arrival was trumpeted by a resounding victory at the 1970 Daytona 200. It also sensationally featured the first disc brakes seen on a mass-produced motorcycle. This machine was a highly visible symbol of the deep-seated Japanese obsession with constant improvement. Honda's huge state-of-the-art manufacturing megalith and a decade of racing dominance were overwhelming. With this bike they simply leap-frogged over the Europeans. The Italian and American industries had to be saved by government. The British fell apart.

Testers tumbled over themselves to find new adjectives to describe the CB750. The term "super-bike" was actually coined to describe it. Like all true classics it has also stood the test of time. The CB750's engineering sophistication and design were a paradigm for the future, spawning a whole generation of Japanese in-line fours. Its close tolerance engineering and horizontally-split crankcase meant it did not drop oil all over the floor, it was quiet and there were no horrible bugs.

The fact that it and its later baby brother, the CB400-Four, destroyed foreign competition has to be seen in an economic context. While it might seem like an evenly-matched fight with Britain coming a close second, that was not the case. It is important to remember that at the time, worldwide production was in the order of 2 million units, whereas the British industry had declined to 20,000 per annum. Thereafter, the world motorcycle market became a Japanese playground.

simple: sell lots of well-made, well-designed bikes to suit people's needs the world over. They fought amongst themselves to win the all-important track and street skirmishes, and they created some true classics. The losers were the European and American manufacturers. For them the 1960s was a litany of under-investment, patronizing dismissal of the opposition and lost chances. Too little, too late. The Japanese ran rings round everyone, and soon they would drive a stake through their hearts.

All hope that the rest of the world's producers could settle into a niche disappeared in 1969. The Honda CB750 was a both masterstroke and a death blow. Its in-line, four-cylinder, 750 cc (45 cu ins) overhead-camshaft engine was hitherto the stuff of

ABOVE: The "Kettle" – the watercooled, two-stroke Suzuki GT750.

Freedom to experiment produced some extra-ordinary machines throughout the early 1970s.

Grand Prix experimentation in the late 1960s led to Kawasaki's introduction in 1969 of a series of mad triple-cylinder two-strokes. The 500 cc (30 cu ins) version, the Mach III, was dubbed the "Widowmaker" because of its mad acceleration and appalling handling. The bike had been conceived specifically to make a name for the recently arrived Kawasaki on the American market. Tuned to blow away the opposition on the traffic-light drag strips of Stateside city streets, it was a wheelie machine without equal. Its acceleration was helped by a spindly frame and forks, hence the foul handling, and a stunningly bad fuel consumption of 18 mpg (6.3 kpg). Suzuki tried a more sedate outlet for its watercooled, two-stroke technology and created a machine dubbed as "the Kettle", the GT750.

The downside of this wild exuberance was that many of the early 1970s bikes were incredibly smokey. Environmentalists attacked them and won. Kawasaki, like Honda, saw the future in the easy-to-tame, four-cylinder four-stroke, but they went further. They came up with an all-time classic, the Z1, soon to be known as "The King". The 900 cc (54 cu ins) double overhead-cam machine was the first riposte to the Honda CB750 and started a power war that is still being fought. Kawasaki had Yvonne DuHamel thrash a specially prepared Z1 round Daytona for twenty-four hours just to prove that this was indeed the King. It had top lap speeds of 256 km/h (160 mph), top speeds of 280 km/h

(175 mph) and set forty-five new world speed and endurance records.

Yet beyond the macho posturing of sports bikes, down the catalogue, in the commuter section, lies a machine still being made thirty-five years after its introduction – the Supercub. This 100 cc (6 cu ins) commuter machine is the true essence of Honda, and Japan's legacy to motorcycling. The 1958 Supercub was the financial platform on which

BELOW: **Pure muscle – the mighty 900 cc Kawasaki Z1.**

ABOVE: **The first edition of the mighty Supercub.**

with plastic so that Mr Average would not know what was going on. But beneath its simplicity was Honda's same high-tolerance engineering and crisp design. This meant that it was virtually bullet-proof – the bike was good for 32,000 to 48,000 km. It also did a remarkable 150 mpg. Mass-production also meant that it was cheap.

In the early 1960s, Honda used the Supercub to radically change the hitherto limited perception of the motorcycle as either a vehicle used for basic transport or a cult item for Hells Angels types. They opened motorcycling up to a vast public. Their advertizing slogan: "You meet the nicest people on a Honda", said motorcycling is clean, it is fun, it is leisure and it is for you. The Supercub's worldwide sales to date have topped 20 million, far-outstripping the VW Beetle. It is designer Soichiro Honda's enduring legacy.

What Honda and the other Japanese makers did that was so different was that they thought to themselves: "What do people actually want to buy?" Many European and British manufacturers were asking: "What do we want to make?" The difference is profound and the gap still exists.

This willingness to give people what they want is why the warrior myth rides on, but now sanitized, plasticized and up-market. The supersteeds for the technological age at a premium price are what we want and we get them, courtesy of Mr Honda.

the whole empire was built. The race replicas may be the eye-catching, headline-grabbers, but the little Supercub is the bulk-produce that has mobilized many countries in the Far East. It is still Britain's best-selling machine.

The Supercub was and is a classic. When it first came out it was seen as an extraordinary object. It was completely new. It was not a motorcycle, and it was not a scooter, yet it combined the benefits of both. It was designed really as a motorcycle for a non-motorcyclist: it was very simple to operate and all the working bits were covered up

A LIGHTER, BRIGHTER FUTURE?

The irony of the Japanese vision is that it now seems that they are actually finding it hard to listen clearly to the customer. While the philosophy of giving us what we want is a sound one, it is being modulated by the needs of such huge manufacturing concerns. There is a sense in which the Japanese have become so confident in their grasp of the problem of motorcycle design that they are travelling down a path of hi-tech complexity without taking stock of what is going on elsewhere. As Honda's flagship model, the Fireblade CBR900, moves towards ever-increasing intricacy of engine design, many outside Japanese design are asking how much longer do we have to put up with the ubiquitous in-line, across-the-frame, four-cylinder, race-replica motorcycle? The answer, interestingly from Europe, is probably not much longer. While they will never sell in anything like the volume of the Japanese, the advances by Ducati, Moto Guzzi and MZ suggest the start of a move towards simplicity. The 900SS, the Daytona and the Skorpion all show a penchant for a lean, hungry, café-racer style, backed by interesting engine layouts, built to Japanese standards. Harley-Davidson have turned their business around to produce motorcycles using

OPPOSITE: The 1991 Yamaha "Morpho" with liquid-cooled, double overhead cam, in-line four engine. Designed with fully adjustable handlebars, footrests and seat to achieve a personalized riding position. A vision of the future?

Japanese methods, while still retaining their legendary Wild West image. They are now successfully marketing heritage and, importantly, responding to an obtuse, but real, love of low-tech design. They have remained true to their traditional values of good, simple engineering. The rapidly improving, next-generation British Triumphs also show there is a desire for change.

However, there are interesting developments which Japan is also moving towards. The increasing lightness of machines is one. The use of immensely strong, hyperlight materials in mountain bikes and race cars suggests that the classic of the future will shed a fair bit of weight. Possible legislation to limit the power output of machines will push it that way too. This is logical and justifiable in a more spartan climate.

But the attention which European and American motorcycles are now getting also shows a need for built-to-last aesthetics. The love of heritage is still very strong.

The future for the Japanese could be in synthesizing the last drop of uniqueness that others retain. One sees in their cars an attempt to ape the Mercedes and the British sportscar of the 1960s.

141

There are many Japanese Harley-Davidson looka-likes. However, it would be exciting if the Japanese manufacturers could rediscover their own lost heritage. The result might be techno-bikes which fuse, for example, Samurai imagery and futurist, urban street cool; they already exist, as a new cult of mythic customization spreads across Japan.

On a broader, more abstract level, if any culture is well-placed to exploit a move towards lightness and simplicity, it is Japan. That country's whole history of admiration for the pure and the minimal is a massive untapped vein for motorcycle designers.

As motorcycling moves into its second century, the potential for change is immense. Looking back, today's classics are bound to be seen as heavy and lumbering, dinosaurs of an over-indulgent culture. But, oh what fun they were!

INDEX